Reflections on Faith and Science from Genesis to Current Events

TS Taylor

All for the Glory of God

Reflections on Faith and Science from Genesis to Current Events

How to Use this Guide v

Biblical Introductions 2

1. Should We Take the Bible Literally......................2

2. What is a Day? Did God Really Create the Universe in Seven Days? 7

3. In the Beginning. Why Does the Bible Start Like This? 12

4. Does the Bible Give True Knowledge or Exhaustive Knowledge? 16

5. Did the Ancients Know Science? Aren't We So Much Smarter Than Them?..............................22

6. Ancient Coroners and Death 27

7. Ancient Life and Death and Miracles, Did They Really Happen? 31

8. Rise From the Dead? Did This Really Happen?35

9. Without Form and Void in Math and Science 42

10. In God's Image or Wholly Other? 45

11. Do Fig Leaves Really Work to Cover Our Shame? 49

12. God's Image – Are Animals Just Like Us? 54

13. Breath of Life. What Does It Mean to Have a Soul? 58

Big Questions.......................................62

14. Spontaneous Generation. Does it Happen Today? 62

15. Is the Universe Expanding?...............66

16. How Can You Independently Measure the Distance to the Stars? 70

17. If God Is Good, Why Is There So Much Evil in the World? 76

18. "That's Not Fair!" Why Does Everyone Know What This Means? 80

19. Is God Fair?......................................84

20. What We Ought to Do. Why Do We Often Struggle with This Idea? 89

21. Does Everyone Go to Heaven?...........93

22. If God Is Sovereign, What is Free Will?............99

23. Blind Trust vs. Evidence-Based Faith..............105

24. Why Do We See the Sky as Blue? 109

25. Abortion Re-Do. What Are the Latest Scientific Ideas on Abortion? 115

26. What Path to Take? How Can We Think About Hard Issues? 121

27. Fossil Formation Questions. A New Way of Thinking 126

28. How Can We Best Think About Fossil Dating?130

29. The Dead Sea Scrolls and Carbon Dating. Why is This Important?...............................135

Technology and Current Events 139

30. What Does God Think about Technology? Is it Good or Bad? 140
31. Who Made the Nails? What Happens When Technology Goes Wrong?...................144
32. Technology That Is Good for the Community..148
33. Dominion Over the Creation. How Are We Doing? 153
34. Why are Utopias so Hard? 157
35. Green Transportation. Are We Close to Achieving This?..163
36. Electric Vehicles - The Good and the Bad.......168
37. Artificial Intelligence, Autonomous Vehicles, and Robots 174
38. Artificial Intelligence and Thinking Machines...179
39. Communication and Making a Name for Ourselves 184
40. The Flow of Information 189
41. How to Best Store Information........194
42. Concluding Thoughts.......................199

How to Use This Guide

Introduction

You may find this reflection guide to be somewhat different from other reflection guides in that its focus is on the intersection of science and the Christian faith. The studies within this book are not meant to be exhaustive, but as a start to a new way of thinking about some perplexing issues.

The main purpose is to present a classic Christian view in light of modern society's view. You might learn some new ideas and some new language that you can use to communicate with your friends and neighbors about who God is and what Jesus has done for us all.

As You Read

Feel free to read these Reflections in any order that you like. You may want to skip over some, you can also go back to them at another time. Feel free to read at your own pace. This is not intended to be an exhaustive study or have deep and complex scientific equations. Therefore, you may want to do some independent research on your own with issues that strike you deeply.

Pray that the Holy Spirit would help the mediations of your heart to be acceptable in God's sight (Psalm 19:14).

Enjoy the questions. They are meant to be open-ended. As such, some of the questions may bring multiple perspectives. If one resonates with you, feel free to ask other deeper questions along the same path.

Personal Study or Small Group?

This book can be used for either personal study or with a small group. If you use it with a small group, think about how best to use your time together.

Pray together. Ask God to open your hearts and minds so that the time together would honor Him and deepen the faith of all involved.

Summarize and discuss. Have one or two people in the group summarize the reflection for this meeting. Ask everyone what they particularly liked (or disliked) about this writing and what was encouraging or challenging.

Questions. Talk through the discussion questions at the end of each reflection. Listen carefully to what others in the group say, as they may be touching on deeper issues. Feel free to allow some questions to take you into a deeper discussion. Also, feel free to table a deeper scientific discussion until another time, to allow those interested to do some more research. Then discuss this at a later time.

Application. How can you use any of these discussions to have deeper conversations about faith with your friends and neighbors? If you have a specific friend in mind, ask others to pray along with you as you seek to discuss your faith more deeply with them.

Rejoice. Above all, rejoice in the richness and majesty of God and how He reveals Himself in His creation.

For more information join us at *https://www.tstaylorbooks.com/*.

Should We Take the Bible Literally?

When it comes to the study of Faith and Science, one of the first questions that often comes to mind is; *"Do you take the Bible literally?"*. Oddly enough, the correct answer to this question is, "Of course, yes." This is because what the question is asking is "Do you take the Bible in the manner in which it was written?" Of course, what other way is there to read any work of literature?

Many people do not realize that the Bible is written in many different literary genres. There is poetry, wisdom literature, didactic literature, and of course historical narrative. Sometimes it takes real work to figure out what literary genre is being used, but with just a bit of careful reading, it is fairly easy to discover the truth.

"¹ The LORD is my shepherd; I shall not want.
² He makes me to lie down in green pastures;
He leads me beside the still waters."
(Psalm 23:1-2)

This is a fairly famous Psalm by King David, written thousands of years ago. David is not trying to convey the idea that God is literally a shepherd in Israel, walking around dusty fields with a flock of sheep. He is giving God human attributes in this way to make it easier for us to better understand who God is and what He is like. David is trying to convey the idea that God loves His people and takes care of His people as a shepherd loves and cares for his sheep. Shepherds are very good at balancing the good of the entire flock with the rescue of one lost sheep. This is also very true with our heavenly Father.

"The proverbs of Solomon: A wise son makes a glad father,
But a foolish son is the grief of his mother." (Proverbs 10:1)

Solomon is giving a pithy couplet to get across the idea of honoring your parents. He compares a wise son to a foolish son. It is meant to be read as a wise saying that is true throughout the ages. This couplet is a typical Hebrew literary technique called parallelism. The verse above is an antithetic parallelism, comparing two different ideas to make a point.

"As vinegar to the teeth and smoke to the eyes,
So is the lazy man to those who send him." (Proverbs 10:16)

This proverb is called a synonymous parallelism, as the two lines convey the same idea in different ways.

13 "You shall not murder.
14 You shall not commit adultery.
15 You shall not steal." (Exodus 20:13-15)

3

Of course, in the Bible, there is the law. A clear description of right and wrong. It is meant to teach us how to live a good and righteous life. Much of modern Western society is based on the laws in the Bible.

Moses is declaring the moral law of God. It is meant to be taken as a rule or a measure of how to live. These laws seem to be an important part of all societies, throughout time and throughout the globe.

"¹Now Moses was tending the flock of Jethro his father-in-law, the priest of Midian. And he led the flock to the back of the desert, and came to Horeb, the mountain of God. ² And the Angel of the LORD *appeared to him in a flame of fire from the midst of a bush. So he looked, and behold, the bush was burning with fire, but the bush was not consumed." (Exodus 3:1-2)*

This is an example of a historical narrative. It gives the name of a real person and how he is related to others at that time. It gives his occupation and his location. It is meant to set the stage for a real event that takes place in space and time. In this historical narrative, God shows up miraculously. The fact that God shows up miraculously, does not negate the truth of the historical narrative.

"For you shall go out with joy,
And be led out with peace;

4

The mountains and the hills
Shall break forth into singing before you,
And all the trees of the field shall
clap their hands. (Isaiah 55:12)

This verse above is clearly Hebrew poetry. This section of Isaiah is expressing the joy of the Creation and what it means to be in a right relationship with God. The image of the mountains singing and the trees clapping their hands is meant to be very dramatic and breathtaking.

So, when reading any part of the Bible, the first step is understanding how the section was written and meant to be read. The next time that you read from the Bible, think about what genre of literature is being used and then read the passage in that context. We will use this literary tool as we go through this study.

Discussion Questions

1. What children's stories are favorites of yours that teach great moral lessons that you don't take "literally"?

2. Can you think of other descriptions of God, like the shepherd? Why do you suppose the Bible uses these different descriptors?

3. Have you ever experienced the mountains singing and the trees clapping their hands, metaphorically? How would you describe that event? How did it make you feel?

4. How can you apply the five W's, Who, What, Where, When, and Why, to better understand a biblical historical narrative? Pick a Biblical story and try it out.

5. What friend would be surprised if you told them the Bible had songs and poems? Why would they be surprised?

What is a Day? Did God Really Create the Universe in Seven Days?

One of the great controversies in Faith and Science is around the creation story in Genesis Chapter 1.

¹ In the beginning God created the heavens and the earth. ² The earth was without form, and void; and darkness was on the face of the deep. And the Spirit of God was hovering over the face of the waters.

³ Then God said, "Let there be light"; and there was light. ⁴ And God saw the light, that it was good; and God divided the light from the darkness. ⁵ God called the light Day, and the darkness He called Night. So the evening and the morning were the first day.

⁶ Then God said, "Let there be a firmament in the midst of the waters, and let it divide the waters from the waters." ⁷ Thus God made the firmament, and divided the waters which were under the firmament from the waters which were above the firmament; and it was so. ⁸ And God called the firmament Heaven. So the evening and the morning were the second day. (Genesis 1:1-8)

The Bible makes it clear that God pre-existed the universe. He created all that is, out of a void that was formless. He started by creating light. He did this by speaking it into existence, "Let there be light". He then went on to create the firmament, the seas, dry land, grass, trees, the sun, the moon, sea creatures, birds, land animals, and finally humans. Each of the creative days ends with a common phrase; "So the evening and the morning were the second day." What exactly does this phrase mean?

The first key idea is the idea of separation, the light from the dark; or day from night. God calls the light good. It is good for many reasons, but one is that it is very important for all life. But He also calls each creative stage "day." What can that possibly mean?

The Hebrew word for day is *yom.* Unfortunately for English speakers, the word *yom* seems to have many uses. In the beginning, *yom* is used for light. Then it is used for evening and morning, implying a day and night cycle.

14 Then God said, "Let there be lights in the firmament of the heavens to divide the day from the night; and let them be for signs and seasons, and for days and years; 15 and let them be for lights in the firmament of the heavens to give light on the earth"; and it was so. 16 Then God made two great lights: the greater light to rule the day, and the lesser light to rule the night. He made the stars also. 17 God set them in the firmament of the heavens *to give light on the earth, ¹⁸ and to rule over the **day** and over the night, and to divide the light from the darkness. And God saw that it was good. ¹⁹ So the evening and the morning were the fourth **day**.* (Genesis 1:14-19)

Then during the fourth creative day, the word *yom* is used repeatedly for daylight as well as for a 24-hour day. This seems to be a bit of a mystery.

For hundreds and hundreds of years all of the great thinkers in the Church; St. Augustine, Francis of Assisi, John Wycliffe, Martin Luther, and John Calvin; to name just a few, all interpreted "evening and morning" to mean a full day cycle, what we would call 24 hours.

After the scientific revolutions in the 1700s and beyond, some Christian thinkers began to relook at the word *yom*. The way that we thought about the solar system and the entire universe began to change, and it forced us to reexamine how we read the opening sections of Genesis. For example, science in the 1700s forced us to examine another Biblical concept – foundations.

Foundations is a tricky word in the Bible. For example, in the Psalms, the Earth is described as having an unshakable foundation:

You who laid the foundations of the earth, So that it should not be moved forever... (Psalm 104:5)

When Galileo and Copernicus turned the scientific world on its head with their idea that the Earth was not at the center of the solar system, but the Sun was, many people would not believe it. How could the Earth be orbiting around the Sun if it does not feel like it is moving? Couple this confusion with the Biblical idea of the foundations of the Earth not being moved, and what is one to believe? All of the early Church fathers like Augustine, Aquinas, all the way up to John Calvin, and Martin Luther believed that the Earth was at the center of the solar system. After all, why wouldn't they if the Earth's foundation could not be moved?

Does the Bible say that the Earth is at the center of the solar system, or is it talking about the glory and power of God as the Creator? How do these ideas get reconciled?

Unfortunately, this serious debate continues. Surprisingly, God does not seem to be too focused on the mechanics of the creation story, but on the purpose of the creation and mankind. Perhaps He is trying to tell us to focus back on "In the beginning God created…"

Discussion Questions

1. Why do you suppose God created all that is? Did He need to do it? Was He required to do it?

2. If you were there with Him during the creation, what would you think and feel about His pace?

3. Could He do it on any timescale that He wanted to? Why or why not?

4. How do these scientific debates relate to the character of God?

5. How do these debates affect your view of your purpose in the creation?

In the Beginning. Why Does the Bible Start Like This?

The Bible begins with;

"In the beginning God created the heavens and the earth." (Genesis 1:1)

It is a rather different opening line for a serious book of literature. You may be more familiar with some other opening lines,

"It was the best of times, it was the worst of times..." A Tale of Two Cities, Charles Dickens (1859)

"It was a bright cold day in April, and the clocks were striking thirteen." Nineteen Eighty-Four, George Orwell (1949)

"It was a dark and stormy night." Snoopy

Most of the time the opening line of a book sets up the period, the place, or the story that is about to unfold. In the Bible, it starts with God existing in the beginning. The story begins to unfold by talking about God. The first thing that we learn is that God existed before the beginning of everything else.

It is very difficult for us to comprehend something or someone pre-existing the universe. For us the universe is everything. It is all matter, energy, and time. It is very hard to grasp that God existed before there was matter, energy, and time. One of the reasons that we know that God must have pre-existed the universe is that science tells us that nothing can spontaneously generate itself. In 1859 Pasteur showed that life does not come from nothing, but typically from pre-existing, smaller organisms that were not previously observed.

The ancient Greek philosophers described it with "οὐδὲν ἐξ οὐδενός" or as we know it in Latin: "*ex nihilo nihil fit.*" Out of nothing, nothing comes. The thinking behind this is that if there ever was "nothing" or "no thing", there cannot ever be any creative matter, energy, or substance to create anything. After all, nothing is nothing! Science is very clear on this.

Yet, the Bible begins with "In the beginning God created..." It does not tell us why God created, but the rest of the Bible tells how God created the world, plants, animals, and humans for His pleasure, and when they were created, "it was good."

The Bible concludes the opening line with; "In the beginning God created the heavens and the earth." The heavens and the earth are a way of describing all that exists. The Biblical account continues with; "The earth was without form, and void, and darkness was on the face of the deep" (Genesis 1:2). This is a really great way of describing the universe before it was created; "form and void and darkness."

The message from the first two verses of the Bible is clear that this is a book about God. It is going to focus on Who He is and What He has done. All through the Bible we will hear the message that we must know who He is before we can truly know who we are.

Take a few minutes to calm your breath, close your eyes, and empty your mind. Imagine that you are a great writer and then imagine the words that you would use to describe the absolute nothingness that was before the universe came into being. All that we know, does not exist, there is only void and darkness. Now imagine a self-existing Creator bringing all that is into existence purely for His great pleasure.

Discussion Questions

1. How do you think He brought everything into existence? Did He shout it, sing it, or just think it?

2. Describe what it would have been like to be there with Him while He created the Earth and all of the creatures.

3. Describe how you would have felt right before He said "Let there be light."

4. How is He still creating today?

Does the Bible Give True Knowledge or Exhaustive Knowledge?

I t has been said that the Bible gives true knowledge but does not give exhaustive knowledge.

Does this strike you as a surprising statement? Does it make sense that the Bible can give true knowledge, but not exhaustive knowledge?

The Bible is fundamentally a book about God. It is about who He is, what He is like, what He loves, and what He hates. Secondarily, it is a book about humans. Who we are, what we should be like, what we should love, and what we should hate. The Bible is written in a way to help us see that we need to know who God is before we can really know who we are.

Given this premise, does the Bible tell us everything there is to know about God? Unfortunately, no. God is so much bigger than we are, we cannot ever totally comprehend Him. After all, what does it mean to be all-powerful and omniscient (all-knowing)? As much as we learn and study, we will never learn all that there is to know about God. For example, God describes Himself as being very far beyond our comprehension;

⁸ *"For My thoughts are not your thoughts,*
Nor are your ways My ways," says
the LORD.
⁹ *"For as the heavens are higher than the*
earth,

So are My ways higher than your ways,
And My thoughts than your thoughts."
(Isaiah 55:8-9)

In its quest to tell us who we are, does the Bible tell us everything that we need to know? Unfortunately, no, the Bible does not give exhaustive knowledge.

For example, in ancient Israel as well as today, a sharp blade is important. It is important to us in the kitchen, to surgeons in the operating room, and to the ancient Israelites in preparing for battle. Accordingly, the Bible talks about the importance of keeping your blade sharp, but it does not tell you how to do that, because even the Israelites did not know how to sharpen their farming tools. God did not tell them and they had not figured it out yet; so, they had to go to their sometimes-enemies, the Philistines, to get their tools sharpened.

19 Now there was no blacksmith to be found throughout all the land of Israel, for the Philistines said, "Lest the Hebrews make swords or spears." 20 But all the Israelites would go down to the Philistines to sharpen each man's plowshare, his mattock, his ax, and his sickle; (I Samuel 13:19-20)

Another area of limited knowledge is angels. The Bible talks a great deal about angels. A good example of this is the famous verse where Gabriel comes to Mary with his big announcement.

26 Now in the sixth month the angel Gabriel was sent by God to a city of Galilee named Nazareth, 27 to a virgin betrothed to a man whose name was Joseph, of the house of David. The virgin's name was Mary. 28 And having come in, the angel said to her, "Rejoice, highly favored one, the   Lord is with you; blessed are you among women!"

29 But when she saw him, she was troubled at his saying, and considered what manner of greeting this was (Luke 1:26-29)

The Bible is pretty clear about some aspects of angels; such as the fact that they exist, they have their own names, and they are frightful in appearance. The Bible tells us what we need to know about angels, but it leaves out an awful lot of interesting facts. For example; How tall was Gabriel? Did he have a body like you and me, or did he have some kind of ethereal body? Did he have wings? If so, what did they look like? God tells us what we need to know about angels, and we can learn the rest when we get to heaven.

Not only does the Bible not tell us everything, it often describes events using phenomenological or descriptive language. For example, what is scientifically wrong with the following passage?

3 From the rising of the sun to its going down

18

The LORD*'s name is to be praised. (Psalm 113:3)*

Of course, the Sun does not move around the Earth so it cannot rise or go down. Copernicus and Galileo convinced us of this idea hundreds of years ago. Yet, surprisingly we still use these same expressions today. Most weather apps today will tell you the exact time that "sunrise" and "sunset" will occur, even though this is scientifically incorrect. Often, we will see phenomenological language in the Bible that is meant to describe the event and it is not meant to give an exhaustive, scientifically correct description. It is a description that works in everyday life.

In the Gospel of Matthew, after Jesus cast out the demons in two demon-possessed men, the multitude that witnessed this act was in awe and shock. They went back to the city and told everyone that they knew.

33 Then those who kept them fled; and they went away into the city and told everything, including what had happened to the demon-possessed men. 34 And behold, the whole city came out to meet Jesus. And when they saw Him, they begged Him to depart from their region. (Matthew 8:33-34)

The scriptures clearly say that "the whole city came out to meet Jesus." Did that mean that every last person in the city; men, women, kids, and little babies came out or is this also a type of descriptive language that is meant to convey the idea that lots and lots of people from the city came out?

As we read through the Bible, we need to get comfortable with what it is trying to tell us with each passage. Sometimes that will mean separating descriptive phenomenological language from historical narrative language. We will also need to become comfortable knowing that the Bible will not tell us everything that we might want to know.

Discussion Questions

1. Do you sometimes wish that the Bible had better descriptions and solutions to some modern-day problems, like a cure for cancer? If you were going to list your top three wishes for better descriptions, what would they be?

2. In the I Samuel verse about blacksmithing, do you suppose the Israelites were frustrated with God that He did not tell them how to do blacksmithing at least as well as the Philistines? Why do you suppose that God did not tell them?

3. Do you get frustrated by your lack of understanding of angelology? How does this lack of understanding affect your view of the rest of the Bible?

4. The expression of the sunrise is a classic example of phenomenological language. Why do you suppose that we still use language like that today, even though we know it is not scientifically correct?

5. What do you think about phrases in the Bible that say "everyone came out?" How do you know how to interpret them?

6. Based on this introductory study, how will you respond to a friend when he or she asks you, "Do you really take the Bible literally?"

Did the Ancients Know Science? Aren't We So Much Smarter than Them?

We often declare today that the Ancients did not know much about science. Nothing could be further from the truth! Our understanding of the Ancients is clouded by our understanding of the Dark Ages. During the Dark Ages, much of what the Greeks had known was lost.

In the 1400s and early 1500s, most people thought that the Earth was flat. This is why the journey of Magellan around the world in 1522 was so significant. He resurrected some very early knowledge of the Greeks.

Not only did the Greeks know that the Earth was round, they actually calculated the circumference of the Earth. In 230 BC Eratosthenes made a very interesting observation. At noon on the summer solstices, the sun was directly overhead of a specific well in the city of Syene. This was quite a sight, as everyone in the town would flock to look down the well and see a perfect image of the sun at the bottom of the well, just one day every year.

One year on the summer solstice, Eratosthenes, was in a different city, Alexandria. He expected to join in the celebration in that city, at their central well. However, instead of finding a central well with no shadow, he found that every building, well, and tower had a shadow. He measured some of the shadows and found them all to be at 7.2°, and not 0°. Eratosthenes thought about this for a while and decided that the only way that this could happen is if Alexandria is "falling away" from Syene. In other words, the Earth is curved and not flat.

Eratosthenes hired a professional walker to walk from Alexandria to Syene. The walker measured the distance between the two cities to be 490 miles. Eratosthenes then calculated the radius of the Earth to be 3,900 miles. This is 98% of the modern value for the radius of the Earth of 3,960 miles. Amazing!

As you can see, Jesus and his disciples grew up in a time of great scientific knowledge and understanding. That is one of the reasons that the narrative of Jesus walking on the water is so significant.

22 Immediately Jesus made His disciples get into the boat and go before Him to the other side, while He sent the multitudes away. 23 And when He had sent the multitudes away, He went up on the mountain by Himself to pray. Now when evening came, He was alone there. 24 But the boat was now in the middle of the sea, tossed by the waves, for the wind was contrary.

25 Now in the fourth watch of the night Jesus went to them, walking on the sea. 26 And when the disciples saw

Him walking on the sea, they were troubled, saying, "It is a ghost!" And they cried out for fear.

27 But immediately Jesus spoke to them, saying, "Be of good cheer! It is I; do not be afraid."

33 Then those who were in the boat came and worshiped Him, saying, "Truly You are the Son of God." (Matthew 14:22-27, 33)

The disciples in the boat were experienced fishermen. Until Jesus showed up in their lives, that was all they knew. They knew the Sea of Galilee like the back of their hands. They knew the properties of buoyance and water density. They knew what floated and what did not. They knew that you could swim in the Sea of Galilee, but you could not walk on top of it.

So, when they saw Jesus walking on top of the water, their first thought was that He was a ghost, because what else could it be? For we know from Occam's Razor that this simplest explanation is often the best. However, in this case; they were surprised that it was a man, Jesus Himself.

Many people in Jesus' time were coming to grips with scientific facts and miracles and how they fit together. They came to see that science did not negate the evidence for a miracle, but helped substantiate the miracle.

Does this discussion help you to see that the miracles in the Bible might make more sense?

Discussion Questions

1. Why do you think that most people today believe that the ancients did not know scientific principles and were basically ignorant?

2. Could you calculate the size of the Earth with just a stick and a protractor? If not, who would you get to help you?

3. If you were in the boat with the disciples, what would you have said when you saw Jesus walking on the water, and why?

4. If your neighbors saw Jesus walking on the water, would it convince them that God is real? Why or why not?

Ancient Coroners and Death

It is often said that the ancients were not very smart, but ignorant and did not know very much about life and science. Nothing could be further from the truth. While the ancients did not have scientific tools that can compare to the modern microscope or telescope, the ancient Romans knew a great deal about life and death.

In the Gospel of John, John tells us about the time that Jesus raised Lazarus from the dead.

38 Then Jesus, again groaning in Himself, came to the tomb [of Lazarus]. It was a cave, and a stone lay against it. 39 Jesus said, "Take away the stone."

Martha, the sister of him who was dead, said to Him, "Lord, by this time there is a stench, for he has been dead four days."

40 Jesus said to her, "Did I not say to you that if you would believe you would see the glory of God?" 41 Then they took away the stone from the place where the dead man was lying. And Jesus lifted up His eyes and said, "Father, I thank You that You have heard Me. 42 And I know that You always hear Me, but because of the people who are standing by I said this, that they may believe that You sent Me." 43 Now when He had said these things, He cried with a loud voice, *"Lazarus, come forth!"* *44 And he who had died came out bound hand and foot with graveclothes, and his face was wrapped with a cloth. Jesus said to them, "Loose him, and let him go." (John 11:38-43)*

Martha, the sister of Lazarus, clearly understood death and the signs of a dead body. Martha had probably been with Lazarus during his last hours on the earth. She probably watched him die. She prepared his body for burial and then placed his body in the family tomb. Lazarus had been in the tomb for four days. Martha was so sure that Lazarus was dead that she warned Jesus of the stench that would come out of the tomb if the stone was removed.

Jesus chose to ignore Martha and her pleas for decency and He ordered the stone that sealed the tomb to be removed. He then called out in a loud voice and brought Lazarus back from the dead. If Martha would have been in the tomb with Lazarus, she would have seen his heart begin to beat again. She would have seen him breathe again. She would have seen his flesh begin to rejuvenate itself and necrosis retreat. There was no question in their minds that Lazarus was dead and now he was alive again.

This narrative is a precursor to Jesus' own death. The Roman soldiers at the cross knew death. The Romans who placed Jesus' body in the tomb knew that they were carrying a dead body. The soldiers who sealed the tomb with a large stone knew that they would never see this person again.

This is why the swoon theory is not a very valid theory. The swoon theory is the idea that Jesus did not really die on the cross, he was just in a swoon. His flogged and crucified body revived itself while he was in the tomb. Without any food, water, or medical attention He recovered so completely that He could move the stone away by Himself. This swoon theory would not win the day in the court of law in ancient Rome, for they knew about death. They knew that Jesus was dead, period.

Discussion Questions

1. Why do you think we have such a dim view of the science (and intelligence) of the ancients?

2. Why do you there are several resurrection stories in the New Testament? Wouldn't one have been enough?

3. Think about what might have happened in the tomb. How would you use science to discuss

the empty tomb with a friend?

4. If you knew that Jesus' resurrection was a hoax what would it be like to pretend that He was alive?

5. How would you walk a modern coroner through the resurrection stories in the New Testament? Would it make a good TV show?

Ancient Life and Death Miracles, Did They Really Happen?

We often wonder, what did the ancients know about death and miracles? The everyday individual in Jesus' time knew so much more about death than we do today. Therefore, they would definitely know a resurrection miracle if they saw one.

While children under one year old do die today, it is not very common. In ancient Roman times, one-quarter to one-third of the children did not live past their first year. Almost all children grew up watching a younger sibling die. Almost all children attended a funeral every year for some young person either in their family or in their village. Children grew up knowing about death.

If they were lucky enough to make it past their first year, they might live to be twenty-five years old, as that was the average life expectance of someone in ancient Rome. While some elders in each village made it into their fifties or sixties; this was rare. Everyone saw death as a common part of everyday life. Everyone participated in preparing a body for burial and designing a funeral service.

This is why the encounter between a particular Jewish religious ruler and Jesus was very unusual. The religious ruler knew that his daughter was dead. He probably watched her die. As other family members were preparing the young girl's body for burial, he rushed out to find this new traveling rabbi, Jesus. When he found Jesus, he told Jesus to

31

come and lay His hands on his daughter so that she would live again.

> ¹⁸ *While He spoke these things to them, behold, a ruler came and worshiped Him, saying, "My daughter has just died, but come and lay Your hand on her and she will live." ¹⁹ So Jesus arose and followed him, and so did His disciples.*
>
> ²³ *When Jesus came into the ruler's house, and saw the flute players and the noisy crowd wailing, ²⁴ He said to them, "Make room, for the girl is not dead, but sleeping." And they ridiculed Him. ²⁵ But when the crowd was put outside, He went in and took her by the hand, and the girl arose. ²⁶ And the report of this went out into all that land. (Matthew 9:18-19, 23-26)*

When Jesus got to this man's house, the funeral procession was in full swing. The professional mourners of the day; the flute players, and the noisy crowd were in the middle of a full performance for honoring the departed girl. Jesus asked for them to make room because the girl was not dead, as He was going to bring her back to life. The mourners laughed at Jesus. They knew death. They knew a dead body. They knew the feel of rigor mortis, the smell; they knew death as a part of everyday life.

Jesus put them outside of the room. He probably spoke to the girl and asked her to take His hand. He then reached out and took her hand and she squeezed His fingers. Her heart started beating, and she started breathing again. After a few moments, she probably opened her eyes and looked at the face of Jesus. They probably smiled together and then she swung her feet off of the bed and got up.

The last line of this story is the most important. "The report of this went out into all that land." Everyone there knew that a miracle happened. Jesus used these miracles as a sign to point to His work with His Father. He came to Earth to do some remarkable things. Everyone there that day knew without a shadow of a doubt that a miracle happened.

Discussion Questions

1. Have you been around death? Would you have been like the Jewish religious ruler and gone out on a limb and publicly asked for a miracle?

2. Why doesn't God do miracles like this every time we ask?

3. Everyone; the professional mourners, the friends of the family, and most importantly the father, knew that Jesus had done a great miracle, the greatest miracle. He brought someone back to life. What does this mean to us today?

4. If you and your neighbors saw a miracle like this, what would everyone think?

5. What does it mean for us today that Jesus did real miracles while He was on Earth?

Rise from the Dead? Did This Really Happen?

A significant keystone pillar of Christianity is that Jesus rose from the dead. This is awfully hard to believe as it is something that just does not occur in everyday life. Matthew sets up the story with:

> *57 Now when evening had come, there came a rich man from Arimathea, named Joseph, who himself had also become a disciple of Jesus. 58 This man went to Pilate and asked for the body of Jesus. Then Pilate commanded the body to be given to him. 59 When Joseph had taken the body, he wrapped it in a clean linen cloth, 60 and laid it in his new tomb which he had hewn out of the rock; and he rolled a large stone against the door of the tomb, and departed. 61 And Mary Magdalene was there, and the other Mary, sitting opposite the tomb.*
>
> *62 On the next day, which followed the Day of Preparation, the chief priests and Pharisees gathered together to Pilate, 63 saying, "Sir, we remember, while He was still alive, how that deceiver said, 'After three days I will rise.' 64 Therefore command that the tomb be made secure until the third day, lest His disciples come by night and steal*

Him away, and say to the people, 'He has risen from the dead.' So the last deception will be worse than the first."

65 Pilate said to them, "You have a guard; go your way, make it as secure as you know how." 66 So they went and made the tomb secure, sealing the stone and setting the guard. (Matthew 27:57-66)

The counterclaims to the stories from Jesus' followers of Him rising from the dead follow a few different paths.

First is that Jesus did not really die. He just swooned in the tomb for three days and during that time His body healed itself and He fooled everyone. Medical science has debunked this idea based on the nature of His death. He was killed by crucifixion, which was the most horrific death for criminals that the Romans could come up with. Crucifixion was a slow and painful death, generally coming from suffocation because the criminal could no longer push his body up to take a breath. In Jesus' case, He was flogged with a cat-o-nine whip so that he was bleeding severely from wounds on His back. Medical science agrees that no one could recover from that in three days with no food, water, or medical attention.

Another idea is that the followers stole His body and then agreed to just make up a story about His resurrection. This does not hold psychological weight in that ten of His original followers were tortured horribly for their faith and not one of them cracked under the torture. Psychologists agree that at least one of them, if not all of them, would have cracked under the pressure. If they knew that the resurrection story was fake, then there was no reason to keep propagating the story of His resurrection. Expect for face-saving, they had nothing to gain from His resurrection stories. They could just go back to their previous employment. For example, Peter was a fisherman. If he could abandon the story of Jesus' resurrection he would get his wife, his family, his job, and get his old life back. However, he held fast to the fact that Jesus rose from the dead. He saw the empty tomb and he saw the resurrected Jesus, multiple times. So, he stuck to the story, even when tortured to death.

Perhaps the most surprising attempt to explain away Jesus' resurrection was from the religious community. The religious leaders, the chief priest, and the elders came up with a plan to bribe the Roman soldiers who were guarding the tomb where Jesus was buried. The soldiers were to tell anyone who asked,

"His disciples came at night and stole Him away while they slept" (Matthew 28:13).

It is incredible to imagine this storyline. These Roman soldiers were some of the best of the best. They would never fall asleep while at their post. Most certainly, they would not all fall asleep at the same time while at their posts. This would be like all of the Secret Service agents guarding a very important person, like a president or vice president, falling asleep on the job. Can you imagine the newspaper headlines the next day? "The President was kidnapped while the Secret Service Agents slept." These agents could never face life again. They could not face their fellow agents, their families, or anyone in the community. It would have been the same for the Roman soldiers. Clearly, this story does not hold water.

Discussion Questions

1. Using Occam's razor, we would have to agree that the simplest explanation for Jesus' resurrection is best. Why or why not?

2. If the most logical explanation is that Jesus actually did rise from the dead, if this is true, what does it mean for your life?

3. Are there other explanations for Jesus' resurrection that make sense?

4. What does it mean if this resurrection story is just a hoax?

Without Form and Void in Math and Science

The opening lines of Genesis are surprisingly chilling:

2 In the beginning God created the heavens and the earth. 2 The earth was without form, and void; and darkness was on the face of the deep. And the Spirit of God was hovering over the face of the waters. (Genesis 1:1-2)

These opening lines start to explain what the universe was like before it was created. Yes, that is quite a brain teaser, describing something before it existed. Obviously, before it existed, it was no thing; nothing. But, how do you describe nothing?

The expression here is "without form, and void." The phrase "without form" is meant to capture the fact that it cannot be described. It has no form, nothing in common with the known physical world. It has no shape, no color, no size, no smell, no taste, and no form. The word "void" is meant to capture the idea of nothingness.

Humans have always had a difficult time with the void, the big Nothing. Even in mathematics, the very clever Romans had so much trouble with the idea of a void that they could not grasp the number zero. They were philosophically opposed to the idea of zero as a number. Every numeral needed to have a set of objects in the physical world that would correspond to the numeral. There was no such object that corresponded to the idea of zero. Hence, there is no Roman numeral for zero, but there are numerals for numbers like 9 and 10; IX, X.

The Romans and the Greeks struggled with the question; "How can not being, be?"

Euclid, the great Greek mathematician, who is credited with the development of geometry, defined things like a straight line, a plane, a triangle, and a point. We all have a working definition of a point. For example, the period at the end of this sentence could be described as a point. However, in Euclid's geometry, a point is described as having no parts or magnitude. It is the punctuation that ends a sentence and at the same time has no dimensions, size, parts, or magnitude. In mathematics, we are still trying to figure out the correct mathematical definition of a point today.

We also struggle with the idea of the void today in astrophysics. As the science of the universe gets more and more complex, the idea of "empty space" recedes further and further into the background.

Space is no longer empty. It is filled with cosmic dust, light photons, neutrinos, gravitons, background radiation, and many other bits of mass and energy. The latest models have most of the universe filled with dark matter and dark energy.

We are not sure what dark matter is, but we think that we know what dark matter is not. It is not a cloud of matter without stars or planets, it is not antimatter, and it is not made up of black holes; yet, whatever it is, it interacts with gravity.

Dark energy is even more mysterious. So far, we know that we cannot detect it, measure it, or taste it. Yet, it seems to permeate all of the known universe in such massive quantities that it makes up about 70% of the entire universe. We believe that space is filled up, but we are still struggling to describe what it is filled up with.

It gets even more mysterious in some of the Big Bang theories, at the very beginning of time; the entire universe started to expand out from a singularity. In the very beginning, it was such a hot ball of energy that the current laws of physics did not apply at all. In fact, when it exploded into being (whatever that means) the light and energy were traveling much, much faster than the speed of light. A very, very short time after the Big Bang explosion, the entire universe was the size of a grapefruit. It makes one wonder, "What was outside this grapefruit-sized universe?" As the universe means all that is, this is quite a brain teaser.

It brings us back full circle to the idea of "without form, and void." Perhaps this language at the beginning of the Bible is much more profound than we originally thought. This idea of "without form, and void" merits much more thought and discussion.

Discussion Questions

1. Take a few moments to draw a picture of "without form, and void". How did you do?

2. If you were to write a song about "without form, and void" how would it go?

3. If you were given a school assignment to write a paragraph description of "without form, and void", what would you write?

4. How would you help a Roman mathematician to understand the idea of zero?

5. If the entire universe was once the size of a very hot and energetic grapefruit, how would you describe what was outside the grapefruit?

6. What do all these thoughts tell us about God the Creator?

7. Based on what you see around you, does it make sense that all of the created world randomly exploded into being? How would you talk about this to a friend?

In God's Image or Wholly Other?

God declares that we are made in His image:

> "26 Then God said, 'Let Us make man in Our image, according to Our likeness; let them have dominion over the fish of the sea, over the birds of the air, and over the cattle, over all the earth and over every creeping thing that creeps on the earth.' 27 So God created man in His own image; in the image of God He created him; male and female He created them. 28 Then God blessed them, and God said to them, 'Be fruitful and multiply; fill the earth and subdue it; have dominion over the fish of the sea, over the birds of the air, and over every living thing that moves on the earth.'" (Genesis 1:26-28)

What does it mean to be made in the image of someone else or to have their likeness? When it comes to humans, we can often see how a baby looks like one or both of his or her parents. We often see the eyes of one parent and the ears of the other on the face of a baby. But, what does it mean to be made in God's image?

Thinkers throughout the ages have quickly discarded the idea that we have eyes or ears like our Creator. For one, we are all too different. For another, He must be so much bigger than us to create all that is.

In general, the great thinkers have come to believe that this means that we are created with intelligence. We are moral agents. We have a conscience. We all understand the concept of fairness. We all have a will and we can execute our wills and desires. We have hearts filled with emotions and passion. We understand what love is, even though we have trouble defining it. We have the ability to create art and beauty and we know how to laugh. All of these characteristics are descriptions of God throughout various parts of the Bible.

However, various theologians have struggled with this idea of being made in God's Image. One in particular, Karl Barth wrote in the early 1900s that God must be "wholly other." Barth argued that God must be so much more intelligent, worthy, holy, loving, etc. than us and that He must be completely different from us. Some have made the argument that God is so far beyond us, He is not a Deity compared to humans, the comparison is more like a human compared to an amoeba. Sure, an amoeba has locomotion and perhaps has a will, but the intellectual gap between humans and amoebas is so great that there is no way in which a human could communicate with an amoeba, nor is there a way in which an amoeba could reach up to a human.

Karl Barth does a great job of expanding on the greatness of God, and His immensity; however, he misses the point that God over and over again tells His people in the Bible that He loves them deeply. Therefore, there must be some connection points between the Creator and the creatures. Because of His greatness, He must be the One to connect with the human. We are too small and unworthy to connect with Him on our own. Therefore, He has reached out over hundreds of years with special prophets, spokesmen, and finally His own Son. This is one of the reasons why the incarnation is such an important concept in the Christian Church.

Modern scientists are beginning to understand just how big the entire universe is. We get a small glimpse of this when we look at all of the stars on a clear night. If God the Creator made all of this, how could we possibly reach out to comprehend Him? A question for the scientist is then, "Just because He must be so much bigger than us, does that mean that He does not exist or we cannot know something about Him?"

Discussion Questions

1. How would the great Creator of all that is choose to connect with His people? What methods would He use?

2. How would you choose to connect with an amoeba?

3. If you were an angel in heaven, and you were given the task to describe God the Creator to humans, what method would you emphasize? Pictures, songs, words, stories, or some other method?

4. How does the vastness of the universe make you feel?

Do Fig Leaves Really Work to Cover Our Shame?

Almost everyone has heard about the fig leaves that Adam and Eve used to cover themselves. The story can be found in Genesis 3:

> *So when the woman saw that the tree was good for food, that it was pleasant to the eyes, and a tree desirable to make one wise, she took of its fruit and ate. She also gave to her husband with her, and he ate. Then the eyes of both of them were opened, and they knew that they were naked; and they sewed fig leaves together and made themselves coverings. (Genesis 3:6-7)*

Eve disobeyed a direct command from God, not to eat from that one tree. There were lots of other trees to eat from, but as we are ought to do, Adam and Eve thought that their freedoms were being impinged on by not being allowed to do what they wanted. They represented us as usurpers. We all rebel against restrictions to our freedom and often we will go out of our way to break any rule that is limiting our lives.

In this case, once they disobeyed God's direct command, they realized their true, rebellious nature and they were ashamed. The word used here is naked, which in this context means totally exposed.

To hide their guilt and shame, they made fig leaf garments to try to cover themselves.

Personal guilt, *I know that I have done something wrong,* and personal shame, *I know that I am a bad person,* are very hard to deal with. Modern psychology has been trying to help us deal with our guilt and shame for a long time, with mixed results.

Sigmund Freud (1856-1939) was the father of psychoanalysis. He thought that our problems of guilt and shame came from deep-seated relational problems with our parents. He proposed that there was also an internal battle between our Id, which is focused on our personal pleasure, our Ego, which helps us deal with reality, and our Superego, which might be thought of as our conscience. While these are helpful insights into some of Freud's ideas, they do not deal with the root problem of our guilt and shame. He did not offer any way to remove our guilt and shame. We all found that our guilt and shame do not go away by just talking about the problem.

BF Skinner (1904-1990) came about 50 years later. He taught that free will was an illusion. Our actions are determined by positive or negative reinforcement. While this was a good philosophy for helping to modify behavior, like in children; he did not help us once we had done something wrong. There is no way to behavior modify guilt and shame away. Again, while these were helpful insights on how we can modify the behavior of others, Skinner did not help us deal with the problem of our own guilt and shame.

Jean Piaget (1896-1980) was a contemporary of Skinner. Piaget was all about education. He believed that education was capable of saving our societies from total collapse. He thought that we could educate proper behavior. Again, while these were helpful insights on how to modify behavior, he did not help us deal with our mistakes. Often, we know what wrong is, but we do it anyway. We have a strong sense of oughtness, what we ought to do in any given situation, yet we cannot always make ourselves do what we ought to do. Piaget's ideas did not help us deal with our guilt and shame.

The story in Genesis continues with God punishing Adam, Eve, and the serpent for their transgressions. After declaring the punishment, He comes alongside Adam and Eve and gives them a way to deal with their guilt and shame. First, he covers them.

Also for Adam and his wife the LORD God made tunics of skin, and clothed them. (Genesis 3:21).

He allows them to cover themselves and then control how they expose their innermost selves to others as they saw fit. We see this in our own lives today. With acquaintances, we allow them to see the high-level, basic parts of our lives. With very close friends, we allow them to see more of our inner lives, even the parts that expose some of our weaknesses and darkness. In our most intimate relationships, we can expose more of our inner selves, but even in these relationships we sometimes hold things back. However, God allows us to share everything about ourselves with Him. If we confess our wrongdoings to Him and ask for forgiveness, He will take our guilt and shame upon Himself and remove it from us. He is able to wash us clean and make us white as snow. God gives us a way to deal with our guilt and shame, He offers to take away from us.

"...Though your sins are like scarlet, they shall be as white as snow; though they are red like crimson, they shall be as wool" (Isaiah 1:18).

God is the only one who can take our guilt and shame and remove it from us "as far as the east is from the west" (Psalm 103:12). Science has been struggling with the problem of guilt and shame for a very long time, with very poor success.

Discussion Questions

1. Have you seen guilt and shame destroy a friend or acquaintance? How would you describe the impact of guilt and shame on their life?

2. How are Freud's psychoanalytic theories still part of our culture today? Do they work today?

3. How would you describe a common method used in society today to cover our guilt and shame? Why does this not work very well?

4. Why does God always tell us that He must help us deal with our guilt and shame? How do verses like Isaiah 1:18 "white as snow" make you feel?

5. What would the world be like if we thought that the weight of our guilt and shame might never be lifted?

God's Image – Are Animals Just Like Us?

When people hear about humans, men and women, being made in God's image, they often ask; "well, what about _____ (fill in your favorite animal)?"

26 Then God said, "Let Us make man in Our image, according to Our likeness; let them have dominion over the fish of the sea, over the birds of the air, and over the cattle, over all the earth and over every creeping thing that creeps on the earth." 27 So God created man in His own image; in the image of God He created him; male and female He created them. (Genesis 1:26-27)

We often talk about special properties that we have; intelligence, passion, creativity, love for art, love for others, our ability to exert our will, and unfortunately our ability to feel shame and guilt.

We often talk about animals that exhibit intelligence. We have seen how smart and caring some animals are like dolphins and elephants. We have seen animals expressing love and concern, especially our dogs and cats. We have seen tool-making in animals such as clever crows. So, what makes us so special? The Bible would describe it as a matter of degree.

In the Book of Isaiah, God describes Himself compared to us like this:

8 "For My thoughts are not your thoughts,
Nor are your ways My ways," says
the LORD.
9 "For as the heavens are higher than the
earth,
So are My ways higher than your ways,
And My thoughts than your thoughts.
(Isaiah 55:8-9)

God is telling us that we have thoughts, important thoughts. We exercise our wills. It is just that His thoughts and His ways are so beyond us, it is like the separation between heaven, where He lives, and earth, where we live.

In the Book of Job, God gives several other clear examples:

4 "Where were you when I laid the
foundations of the earth?
Tell Me, if you have understanding.
5 Who determined its measurements?
Surely you know!
Or who stretched the line upon it?
6 To what were its foundations fastened?
Or who laid its cornerstone,
7 When the morning stars sang together,
And all the sons of God shouted for joy?
(Job 38:4-7)

God makes it clear that He made the universe and the earth with great care. He laid the foundations. He measured it to make sure it was right. He created the stars and galaxies so that they may sing to God's glory. Yes, we can create things, but can we create an entire universe?

"Can you bind the cluster of the Pleiades, Or loose the belt of Orion? (Job 38:31)

A little later on in the discourse, He challenges Job to undo (loosen) the belt of Orion. Orion is a huge wintertime constellation that dominates the night sky. It is made of many different stars. The belt is made of three stars that appear to be in a straight line. God tells us all something like; *If you think you are so great, make another Orion in the sky.*

God uses these descriptions to help us understand that He is vastly different from us. In the same way, we have things in common with the animal kingdom; yet we are vastly different from them.

When the animals look at the stars at night, do they contemplate the constellations and ponder Orion's belt? Do they ponder the foundation of the earth? Do they ponder the size of the universe or how long it has existed? Do they see the stars singing together? Do they see beauty in a spectacular sunrise? Do they contemplate what it will be like to live on the planet Mars?

These are small pieces of what it means to be made in God's existence.

So, enjoy your relationships with your animal friends, but more important; consider what it means that all men and women are made in God's image.

Those that you love, those you do not like, and those whom you hate. They are all made in God's image. If you really believed this, how would you live your life differently?

Discussion Questions

1. Imagine that you see a friend out walking their dog. How would you describe to them how uniquely they are made in the image of God, so much more than their dog?

2. How would you describe how much more is God's love for your friend than their love for their dog?

3. Can you think of people whom you know (and maybe don't like) that God might want you to reflect His love to? How could you do that practically speaking? How might this impact them, and you?

The Breath of Life. What Does It Mean to Have a Soul?

I n Genesis Chapter 2, the creation of Adam is described using:

"And the LORD God formed man of the dust of the ground, and breathed into his nostrils the breath of life, and man became a living being." (Genesis 2:7)

Everyone wonders what the "breadth of life" means. It is a bit difficult to understand because it is an old Hebrew expression and there are several aspects of this expression.

First, we see that God Himself breathed into the man so that he might become a living being. God could have just had the four winds blow into the man, or He could have given him a sharp spanking. However, God did something much more personal, He breathed into his nostrils. This is an expansion of what it means to be made into the image of God (Genesis 1:27). God did something special to the man and by extension to all of us by giving us the breadth of life.

Another understanding of the verse is to see the idea of body and soul. We are not just physical creatures, nor are we just intellectual or spiritual creatures. The idea of body and soul was a big problem for Greek philosophers. According to Plato, the soul gave us reason, spirit, and appetites. The soul was the life driver for us all. At times, Plato abhorred the physical body as it was often in conflict with the soul.

These ideas of Plato are still very much alive today, in our modern world views. At times we hate our bodies. They are not what we want. They are too big, too small; too fat, too thin; they are too weak, too inflexible; their desires are too strong, and they often lead us astray.

For example; our spirit or mind or soul keeps telling us to stay away from the temptation, like the next drink or drug; but our body is too weak and we cave to the temptation. Like in Plato's time, we live with our spirit in conflict with our bodies.

The view in Genesis is quite different in that there is complete unity between body and spirit. God made both and He gave us both. Sometimes, God's creative activity is described as a potter forming a vessel out of clay. The Potter meticulously forms the vessel for a specific purpose. Not all vessels are the same, they do not look the same, but they each have their own specific purpose. When God created us, He created us to be engaged in purposeful activities, and through these, we would find our meaning. The spirit needs the body and the body needs the spirit.

Then Darwin came along with his evolutionary theory. In his theory, we all evolved from the primordial goop. Today we see that we not only share a lot of DNA with the apes, but we share DNA with fruit flies. The explanation is that as we have a great deal of commonality, therefore, we must all be the same.

There are two major weaknesses to this theory. The first is that just because there is a great deal of commonality does not necessarily mean that we are all the same. After all, we are all carbon-based organisms, so it only makes sense that we would have a great deal of commonality. We would expect to have less commonality with nitrogen-based organisms.

The second weakness is around the idea of body and soul, or body and spirit. We cannot wrap our heads around the idea of bacteria or viruses having a soul. They do not seem to have a complex enough body to house a soul. So, that brings up a host of questions:

- Which organisms have a soul?
- Where did this soul come from?
- Did it just randomly happen one day? If so, how does a random event like this have any meaning?
- Plato had the idea that the soul outlived the body. What would Darwin think about this?

The idea of the soul and the conscience was very troubling for Darwin. He could not figure out how the conscience could randomly evolve. Darwin has no answers to the perplexing questions above, and the still stump many scientists today.

It seems that the Judeo-Christian idea of the breath of life better answers many of these questions and most clearly answers some of the big questions.

Discussion Questions

1. If you were given the debate question, "In Darwin's evolutionary theory, when did the soul come into existence?", describe your approach to answering this question.

2. How do you put together the ideas of body and soul?

3. Do you see the conscience as a good thing for humans? If so, why or why not?

4. What do you think of the idea of your soul living after your body? What excites you about this idea?

Spontaneous Generation. Does It Happen Today?

The early Greek philosophers, like Aristotle, thought deeply about a wide range of subjects. One particularly thorny issue was *where does life come from?* Without the aid of modern microscopes, it was easy to surmise that some organisms came directly out of the sand and mud. For example, Aristotle believed that scallops came directly out of the sand. The general thesis was that life comes from non-life and that no causal agent was required. This seemed to explain a great deal of the world; especially some of the nastier creatures like fleas, mosquitos, and maggots. For most certainly maggots seemed to come directly out of decaying fish.

The idea of spontaneous generation survived for thousands of years. Even the early Christian thinkers, such as St. Augustine, believed that spontaneous generation was described in some of the creation verses; such as "Then God said, 'Let the waters abound with an abundance of living creatures...'" (Genesis 1:20a). After all, the descriptive language seemed to say that creatures just came out the waters.

In the 1600s, the scientist Jan Baptist van Helmont did some interesting experiments with plants and mice. He planted a willow tree in a planter with a known amount of soil. He measured the growth of a willow tree for five years and compared its growth in mass to the loss in the mass of the soil. As the soil lost very little mass during this time, he concluded that the tree was spontaneously generating itself. He also concluded that mice could spontaneously generate from wheat scraps that were left in the garden shed. Aristotle's early ideas were very much entrenched in everyone's thinking.

In the mid-1800s Louis Pasteur became very interested in the idea of spontaneous generation. He found that boiling meat could prevent the growth of mold and spores and he eventually concluded with two significant ideas. One, there seem to be many small creatures (bacteria) living in decaying pieces of meat, and two, boiling them could kill them. Pasteur did several things for science. One he helped us to begin to understand microscopic life, like bacteria. Second, he killed the idea of spontaneous generation, once and for all. From the mid-1800s to the mid-1900s spontaneous generation was dead and buried.

Much to the surprise of many scientists, spontaneous generation came back to life along with the theory of the Big Bang. The Big Bang is often described as the universe *exploding into being.* It explodes out of nothing. Unfortunately, science has said for over one hundred years that this cannot happen.

This is quite a quandary for the scientific idea of the Big Bang. Where did the Big Bang come from? What started it? If there was a singularity with no mass or energy, how could the universe be formed from this starting point? These are interesting and difficult questions.

The famous British physicist, Stephen Hawking, is purported to say that before the Big Bang, there was absolutely nothing. This is quite an interesting scientific and philosophical quandary. Is spontaneous generation back on the table?

Perhaps "In the beginning God…" is beginning to make scientific sense.

Discussion Questions

1. Have you ever thought about what makes food spoil? In light of this, how do you make sense of the theory of spontaneous generation?

2. If a friend told you that the universe "exploded into being", what would you say?

3. What would you say if a scientist said that "We do not know what existed before the Big Bang. It is outside of the realm of science? Why would you still say that this is an important discussion to have?

Is the Universe Expanding?

I n the 1950s scientist started to be excited about the idea that we now call the Big Bang. The idea came from observations from great earth-bound telescopes. The idea got stronger scientific backing after the Hubble Telescope that was launched into low-earth orbit in 1990. Since then, more and more data seem to say that the universe is expanding.

This seems to squash the Steady State Model of the 1970s that said that the universe as we see it today is the way that it has always been. The Steady State Model made a lot of sense to many scientists because they like consistency. There are many natural laws like the law of gravity, the law of the conservation of energy, and the absolute of the speed of light that were decreed to be the same for all time and all places. This felt good and made some of the science easier to understand.

When more and more deep space observations observed the "red-shift" in other stars and galaxies, it seemed like the universe was not in a steady state condition, but it was expanding. The next big question was; "Is the universe expanding and then contracting or is it continually expanding?" The cyclical universe was again in a more comfortable position because it did not have to deal with the gnarly question of the beginning. If the universe has existed for all time, just expanding, then collapsing, and then expanding again; there was no need for a creator God.

Unfortunately, in the 1990s the deep-space telescopic data seemed to say that the universe was expanding at an ever-increasing rate. The great hope was that the gravitational force from all of the stuff (matter) in the universe would pull hard enough on the other stuff to keep it mostly together. That does not seem to be the case.

Scientists are trying to understand what could cause this great acceleration. There is no clear understanding, but there is a general consensus that there must be a lot, I mean a whole bunch of a lot of dark energy and dark matter. The latest consensus is that 70% of the entire universe is made up of dark energy and about 25% is made up of dark matter. Hence only 5% of the known universe is made up of regular matter. The rest is a mystery. Dark matter is an unknown material that is not like any other material in the universe, except that it seems to be able to affect the known universe in an understandable way with the force of gravity. Dark energy, which is most of the universe, is totally unknown. Scientists do not know what form it takes; if it has mass associated with it, if it has charge or spin, or if it is pure energy. It is a total unknown, but it must exist to make the math behind the expanding universe work out.

Unfortunately, this stage of science sounds a bit like some of the musings of Isaac Newton and others about how light could travel from the sun to the Earth. In the 1700s a substance called the ether was hypothesized as a medium for the transmission of light in a vacuum. In other words, the vacuum of space was not empty, it was filled with ether. The ether was there so that light could move throughout the universe. The ether model lasted for over one hundred years before some important scientific experiments disproved the presence of the mysterious ether. It turned out that light did not need the ether to move throughout the universe.

This is how science works. Theories are hypothesized, tested, and modified until they are finally disproved and replaced with something else, or they are morphed into a more modern theory. Unfortunately, during the brawling time of refining a theory, too many ideas are presented as "scientific facts." Scientific facts need to be proven in a repeatable way. Many of the current theories surrounding the Big Bang are just that, theories. Unfortunately, in our "sound bite" communication world today, there is great confusion between scientific facts and scientific theories.

Discussion Questions

1. Study what assumptions might be wrong with any of the current scientific theories, for there are probably many, many weak or false assumptions. Why do weak assumptions matter in any discussion?

2. What does this tell you about scientific fact versus scientific theory?

3. What is the difference between belief in an unproven scientific theory and faith?

4. What is the difference between knowing something and believing something? For example, what do you know about the solar system and what do you believe?

How Can You Independently Measure the Distance to the Stars?

When you look up into the night sky, how do you know how far any star is away from you? Is a brighter star necessary closer? Is a larger star necessary closer? Not necessarily, because big and bright could be either far away, or close by, or somewhere in between.

It would be nice if some of these variables could be better understood. Fortunately, some techniques can be used.

For stars that are fairly close by (about 10,000 light-years), an old technique, called parallax can be used to measure their absolute distance from the Earth. We use parallax every day with our stereoscopic vision that comes from our two eyes that are spaced apart. The trick with telescopes is to use the orbit of the Earth around the sun to provide a stereoscopic view of the sky. Astronomers take pictures of the sky in the springtime and then take the exact same picture in the fall with the Earth on the other side of the sun. This parallax motion of the Earth can be used to help us calculate an absolute distance measurement to some stars.

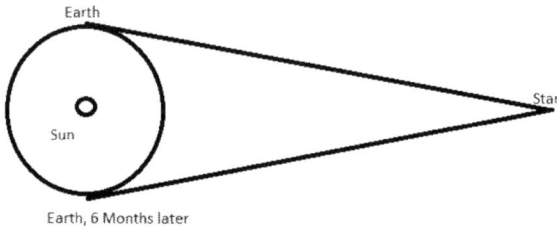

Earth

Sun

Star

Earth, 6 Months later

Victory in measuring the distance to the stars was declared until we realized that there are some pretty big assumptions being made when estimating the distance to other stars that appear to be very far away. The first assumption concerns the parallax method. While the orbit of the Earth around the Sun is big, it is really quite small compared to the expected size of the universe. By using really sensitive measurements, we estimate that we can use parallax for stars about 10,000 light-years away. While 10,000 light-years is a long way, it is still very small when used to extrapolate to 10 Billion light-years.

For stars that are further away, up to about 200,000 light-years, the color, temperature, and true brightness can be used to estimate the distance to the stars. A spectroscope can be used to measure the color of the star. From this color, we can assume the temperature of the star; as here on Earth a blue flame is hotter than a red flame. If we assume this holds true for all stars, even those that are over 100,000 years old, we can determine the true brightness of the star. When we look through a telescope, we see the apparent brightness of the star. The apparent brightness will vary with the distance, using the inverse-square law. That is, if one star is twice as far away as another, it will be one-fourth as bright. By comparing the true brightness to the apparent brightness, we can estimate the distance to stars up to about 200,000 light years away. This of course assumes that our true brightness assumptions hold for stars that might be 200,000 years old.

Around 1908 Henrietta Swan Leavitt discovered some variable (pulsing) stars in the nearby Magellanic Clouds. For these pulsing stars, known as Cepheid stars, the longer the pulsation period, the higher their absolute magnitude of brightness. Henrietta's discovery gave us a way to estimate the absolute brightness of some stars, that are not nearby, but as much as ten million light-years away.

The other underlying assumption is that all of the rules that apply to the stars that are close by apply to the stars that are very far away. This is a fairly fragile assumption given what we hypothesize about the Big Bang.

At the beginning of the Big Bang, none of the laws of physics applied, even the absolute value of the speed of light. Many Big Bang scientists believe that it took a bit of time for things to settle down to the four basic laws of physics; strong, weak, electromagnetic, and gravity. Even in the beginning, much of the Big Bang material was moving away at speeds much greater than the

72

speed of light. However, given this, the underlying assumption is that the universe settled down in exactly the same way, all around. What's to say that the "right" side of the Big Bang, didn't develop with slightly different variations of the basic laws from the "left" side? This would make it very difficult to extrapolate the same laws to various parts of the universe. The second side of this same assumption is that the laws that we use to measure the distance to faraway stars apply even though these stars are potentially billions and billions of years back in time. Who is to say that the laws were not different back then?

This line of thinking leads us to two different thoughts. The universe is believed to be very uniform, even though the chaotic formation of the laws of physics would seem to go against this uniformity. This leads us to ask *"Why should the universe be uniform"?* The second thought has to do with the old Hebrew law of independent verification, that is having two witnesses.

"Whoever is deserving of death shall be put to death on the testimony of two or three witnesses; he shall not be put to death on the testimony of one witness."
Deuteronomy 17:6

Independent verification, or two witnesses, is important in much of life. Therefore, we are still trying to figure out an independent verification method for stars that appear to be really far away. We have yet to come up with any really good independent verification methods.

Discussion Questions

1. Think about many of the basic assumptions that we make in science in the everyday world and what they tell us about our basic views of the construct of the world. Are there ideas that we just believe without having any scientific proof? Name a few.

2. Can you come up with two independent ways for measuring the distance to an object that is billions of light years away?

3. Describe in time in your life when you got someone to independently verify a story.

4. How is the independent verification model important in our court system today?

5. Do you think that independent verification is important in science today?

If God is Good, Why is There So Much Evil in the World?

The question of good and evil has plagued serious thinkers for thousands of years. On the one side, we have an all-powerful, all-loving God and on the other side, we have a world filled with evil deeds, evil people, and natural disasters. It would seem that God is either not good or He is not all-powerful.

Let us first address the all-powerful issue. Is there anything that God cannot do? Of course, there are lots of things that God cannot do. He cannot exist and not exist at the same time. He either exists or He doesn't. Can a good God do evil, can He do things that go against His own nature? No, He cannot do that either. If lying is a sin, God cannot sin. For example, He can only tell the truth and He must keep all of His promises. He cannot break a promise to His people.

Is God good, loving, and filled with lovingkindness? This is trickier to answer because we all may have different views of what good is. For example, your teenage daughter may think that it is good that she goes to a party because "everyone else is going." You, as a parent, may not think that it is good for her to go to this party as it is advertised to have lots of illegal drugs and alcohol. In general, the standard of good is decided by the higher authority, such as the parent in this case. While it may not be the best way to define what good is, it has occurred this way in society for millennia.

God had given us some standards of good with laws on how we should interact with each other. We are not to murder each other, we are not to steal from one another, we are not to have sex with someone else's spouse, we are not to slander or lie in public about each other, and we are not to be consumed with the desire for things that are not ours (Exodus 20:13-17). Jesus went on to expand on these to say that the correct standard of goodness is to not only not do these things but to not even have them dwell in our hearts and minds. For example, just thinking hateful thoughts about someone else is akin to murder (Matthew 5:21-26). To be good like God means to never do these acts or even think about them. This is indeed a high standard indeed.

From this, we see that God's own standard of good far exceeds our own standard of good. From this, we can see that some of the evil in the world comes from us. We are not good, as measured by God, none of us are. If some of the evil in the world comes from us, why doesn't God just wipe us out when we commit an evil act? It seems that God stays His righteous judgment because of His mercy.

"The Lord is merciful and gracious, slow to anger, and abounding in mercy." (Psalm 103:8)

He is waiting for us to come to Him, to ask for His forgiveness, and then to ask for His help with our lives to better model a good life.

Bad things also come in the form of natural disasters. Why do these happen and why do "good" people get killed in them? We see from the discussion above, there are no "good" people. Some are much worse than others, but none of us are good. Still, why does anyone get killed in a natural disaster? Jesus addressed this issue with the people of His time. There was a construction project going on in the area of Siloam, just outside the city walls of Jerusalem. One of the towers fell and killed eighteen people. Jesus said that these people were no more innocent or evil than anyone else. He uses this as a warning to everyone that we could also be killed today or tomorrow; in a traffic accident, falling down the stairs, or in a drive-by shooting. Jesus says, "Unless you repent you will all likewise perish" (Luke 13:1-5). Jesus is driving home the point that God is very merciful with us all when He does not deal with us as we deserve. He wants us to reevaluate our lives and turn back to Him. Perhaps these natural disasters are God speaking to us not with a whisper, or with a normal voice, but shooting with a megaphone. He is trying to get our attention.

Discussion Questions

1. What does it take in your life for God to get your attention?

2. How has God used pain and suffering in your life to get your attention?

3. How was your life changed afterward?

4. How was it during the dark times?

"That's Not Fair!" Why Does Everyone Know What This Means?

We all seem to have an insatiable need to see others play fair, for justice to prevail. We see it when someone cuts in front of us, when they take the last item on the plate, and even when the courts come up with a verdict that we do not agree with.

Where does this desire for fair play and justice come from? Ever since Darwin's Evolutionary Theory, scientists have been trying to place it. Science first started to deny the need for fair play and justice, but it did not get very far. Everyone saw the need for fair play and justice in their lives. They saw it no matter what their socioeconomic group or where on the globe they lived. Everyone everywhere seemed to have a sense of fair play and justice. While they agreed that the details of what is fair varied somewhat for different people, the sense of fair play is always there.

This was even more clear when children were studied. All children, everywhere seem to understand the idea of fair play, especially when they thought someone else was not being fair to them. They did not need to be taught this idea of fair play, they seemed to know what it was from the beginning. If someone accused them of not playing fair, they all seemed to know what that meant, even if they did not like it.

The scientists then dug deeper into Darwin's theory of the survival of the fittest. There seemed to be a strong correlation between the sense of fair play and the theory of the survival of the fittest, except that it was a two-sided coin. Sometimes they saw that people pushed for fair play and justice because it improved their place in their society. It moved them up in the hierarchy and hence gave them a better chance of being one of the fittest.

However, there are always times when the sense of fair play required them to give up something, perhaps their elevated position. Oddly enough they would sometimes give up their elevated position to satisfy their sense of fair play.

The hardcore Darwinists could not make heads or tails out of the sense of fair play. If we all come from the same primordial goop, there cannot be any sense of right or wrong or fairness in the universe. For we know that information cannot come from random processes. Chance has no way of understanding or producing a standard of justice. This leaves our Darwinist friends in a tough spot. Either our sense of fair play and justice does not exist, which does not jive with our view of ourselves, or there is some kind of Intelligent Design behind the creation of all.

St. Paul talked a bit about this in his letter to the Church in Rome.

"[The Gentiles] who show the work of the law written in their hearts, their conscience also bearing witness, and between themselves their thoughts

accusing or else excusing them... (Romans 2:15)

Paul talks about God writing His basic law on the hearts of everyone. He describes this written law as their conscience. Perhaps this is a better way to describe the origin of our need for fair play.

What do you think of this dilemma for Darwin's theory?

Discussion Questions

1. How would you talk to a Darwinist friend about the paradox of our sense of justice and the idea that there can be no justice from a random beginning?

2. Why don't our children need to be taught the idea of fair play?

3. If children know what fair play is, why is it so hard for them to do it?

4. How can you help a child to play fair? Would you use the same method on an adult? Why or why not?

Is God Fair?

Words are hard. It is often difficult to understand what is meant by the usage of common words, like fair. What does it mean to be fair?

Two words that are confusing today are equality and equity. They are related to each other and to the concept of fairness, but they have very different meanings. Equality means that each person or group of people is given the same resources or opportunities. Equity means that there is an equal outcome.

For example; imagine a kid's baseball game. Equality means that each team has the same number of players, uses the same bats and balls, and they have the same scoring rules. It is a fair game. However, one team is much better than the other, so the score at the end of the game is 10 to 1. Equity means that the same two teams play the same game with the same scoring rules; but at the end of the game, the score of 10 to 1 is changed to a score of 10 to 10. It is an equal score. This is not the same as equality. Which is fair?

As another example, imagine government equity. Government equity is when the government takes from some (using taxes) to give to others (the needy) to make everyone more equal (have the same). This is easy for most of us as the government generally takes from others, those richer than us, and gives to others or ourselves. We generally think that this is fair because it does not usually negatively impact us and sometimes it benefits us directly.

Now imagine personal equity. You see a hungry, homeless person on the street and so you take them to your bank and you give them half of what is in your bank account. This is personal equity in action. We generally do not do this as it is much harder.

Which of these is fair?

When we talk about God, we often use other words, such as justice and mercy. Justice means doing the right thing. For example; imagine one person who murders another person out of pure hatred and spite because the other person has more money or property. In another example, a person steals a loaf of bread to feed their children. They both did wrong, but do they deserve the same punishment? What is justice?

Mercy is something that is by definition not required. It is a free gift. For example, you see someone doing a random act of kindness to someone else in the grocery store parking lot. It is a pure act of mercy. Are they then required to do the same act of kindness for you? Do you feel good watching them do this act of kindness to someone else? How do you feel when they don't do the same act of kindness for you?

Now, is God fair?

God treats us with equality in that we are all given the desire to live a purpose-filled life. God has made us unique individuals, so in that sense, we are not all equal. Some of us are smarter, stronger, faster, or taller than others; yet He has given us all the ability to love Him and others, in our own unique way.

In that sense, God is just and fair.

God is also merciful. He gives some of us a second chance in life when He does some great act to get our lives back on track. He pulls us back from the brink of destruction. Is He required to do this? No. Is He merciful when He does this? Yes. Do we make good use of His mercy? Sometimes yes. However, sometimes no, as we waste the opportunity.

Is God fair? Yes, He is just. He does the right thing always, as He loves doing the right thing. Is God merciful? Yes. He loves being merciful at times. Is God required to be merciful? No. Mercy is not required, just as random acts of kindness are not required. If they were required, they would not be random acts.

The Bible talks a great deal about God and His mercy and justice. The Bible describes God's gracious nature as One who waits. It also tells us that God is a God of justice. He asks that we would wait for Him, to forgive us when we acknowledge our wrongdoings and when we need His direction in life.

*Therefore the LORD will wait, that He may
be gracious to you;
And therefore He will be exalted, that He*

may have mercy on you.
For the LORD is a God of justice;
Blessed are all those who wait for Him.
(Isaiah 30:18)

For example, God expects us all to love Him and to love our neighbors. Is that fair?

36 "Teacher, which is the great commandment in the law?"

37 Jesus said to him, "'You shall love the LORD your God with all your heart, with all your soul, and with all your mind.' 38 This is the first and great commandment. 39 And the second is like it: 'You shall love your neighbor as yourself.' (Matthew 22:36-39)

Discussion Questions

1. What did you think about the discussion on equality vs. equity? Is God focused on equality, equity, both, or neither?

2. Has God always been fair to you? Did it always feel that He was fair?

3. How should we respond when He does things that do not <u>feel</u> fair?

4. God expects us all to love Him and to love our neighbors. Is that fair?

What We Ought to Do. Why Do We Often Struggle with This Idea?

We often struggle with the question of what we ought to do. Is this the right path or should I take another? Why did I not do the right thing? We all have struggled with the question; "What should I do?"

This was also a big question for Charles Darwin. He struggled with the idea of conscience. The thing inside us that tells us about right and wrong, or what we ought to do. He could not figure out how to put the conscience into his Evolutionary Theory. He knew that he had a conscience because he had felt its sharp barb on his mind numerous times, yet he could not figure out how it fits into the survival of the fittest. The conscience seems to drive us to go against the basic nature of the survival of the fittest. In fact, in extreme cases, that internal "ought to machine" would drive us to sacrifice ourselves for the good of someone else. Darwin could not understand how to place this into his theory.

He knew that rocks and trees did not have any "ought to machine." He knew that if you dropped a rock, it would fall according to the law of gravity, regardless of its personal feelings on the subject. The rock did not first figure out that it ought to fall, it just fell. The same goes for trees. They did not figure that they ought to grow straight and tall. If they had good soil and sunlight, they just grew straight and tall.

It is not so with us. We sometimes do what we ought to do, but often we do the opposite. In the Bible, God says,

"Let Us make man in Our image, according to Our likeness..." Genesis 1:26.

Being made in the image of God means that we have the ability to reason, think, feel, and create. It also means that we have the ability to know good and then to strive to always do good. Unfortunately, as fallen creatures, we often miss the mark of doing good.

In the story of Adam and Eve, they disobeyed God and ate the fruit in the garden. They knew they had done wrong and so they hid from God.

8 And they heard the sound of the Lord God walking in the garden in the cool of the day, and Adam and his wife hid themselves from the presence of the Lord God among the trees of the garden.

9 Then the Lord God called to Adam and said to him, "Where are you?"

10 So he said, "I heard Your voice in the garden, and I was afraid because I was naked; and I hid myself." (Genesis 3:8-10)

When we know that we have not done the right thing, we often feel shame and guilt. Darwin could not figure out how shame and guilt fit into the survival of the fittest. Shame and guilt often only slow us down and make us less productive. We often feel bad about ourselves and it is even harder to go on and do the right thing.

Not only could Darwin not place these ideas into his Evolutionarily Theory, but he also could not understand how to make guilt and shame go away. He did not observe the rocks or trees or birds struggling with guilt and shame, these seemed to be strictly a human condition. Where did these ideas come from? It seems that life would be much simpler if we did not have a conscience, a sense of oughtness, or guilt or shame. Ultimately, Darwin had to conclude that these concepts must have something to do with us being made in the image of God. God must be the source of our striving to do what we ought to do, even if it puts us personally at a disadvantage.

Discussion Questions

1. What do you think about the "ought" to machine in your life? Do you sometimes wish that you could turn it off?

2. When you make a mistake or do something you ought not to do, do you feel guilt and shame? What do you do with your guilt and shame?

3. Does this feeling of "I ought to do something" make us a better person? Why or why not?

Does Everyone Go to Heaven?

This is a very common, simple question in society today; but it has many complicated assumptions behind it.

First, what is heaven? It is generally thought to be a good place where God lives. It is generally viewed as not so much a physical place, but a spiritual place. This of course assumes that God exists. If we assume that God exists, we must know something about Him to understand the rules of heaven.

For God and heaven to make any sense, we must assume that God lives forever, that is He doesn't die and He is eternal. He must also live outside of the physical world, to have a place for us to go to after we die. Based on this, it would make sense that He existed before the physical universe, as He stands outside it; hence He must be the Creator. We can think of heaven then as His place and as His place, He sets the rules and parameters.

For us to live in heaven, we must have a spiritual side to our being, which we generally call our soul. The soul is a big part of us, but separate from our physical side. Our soul embodies our personality, our will, our emotions, or as we say – who we are. However, if we are tall, is our soul tall? Does our soul match our skin color? What language does our soul speak and understand? Questions like this and many more like them have perplexed mankind for many centuries.

Does our soul live on past our physical bodies? Yes, that seems to be implied in the question about heaven. Does our soul live on forever? As we have not been there, we cannot know for sure; but it would seem that as it is His place, God would set the rules about this.

To answer the question, we must assume:

- God exists
- Heaven is a spiritual, non-physical place where He reigns
- Only our soul would go there
- As it is His place, He sets all of the rules about the place

Over the centuries there are been several views about heaven:

1. Everyone goes there after they die
2. Most people go there, based on their good works outweighing their bad works
3. Some people go there, based on their religious affiliation
4. Some people go there, based on their relationship with God

The problem with the idea of everyone going to heaven is that it would not be any different from life here on earth, except we would live longer. There would still be people who would want more power and possessions than they have at the present time. This would lead to strife and perhaps wars, so it would end up being much like the world today, which is generally a bit of a mess. All of us can envision people that we would not want to live with forever, so we would not want them in our heaven. Unfortunately, there are probably some people who would not want *us* in heaven. A heaven with everyone in it does not seem to be a very good idea.

That quickly leads to the second idea, that only "good" people get to heaven. Or said differently, really bad people would not get in. Most of us cannot conceive of really bad people like Hitler or Stalin or (fill in the blank of your most hated person) being with us in heaven. This leads to the idea that you have to be "good" enough to get into heaven. Of course, we all think that we are good enough, we are just not sure about others. However, we should probably not be the standard of good enough; because we know that deep inside, we are often selfish, envious, hateful, spiteful, overly proud, conceited, untrustworthy, and generally unloving. Paul gives a pretty good list of our shortcomings in his letter to the Church in Rome (Romans 1:28-32). We should not get to set the standard of "good" enough. God gets to set it; so, what does that mean?

This has led to the idea that if you are a member of the right religion, you would get into heaven. Roman Catholicism, Islam, and Judaism, for example, are all monotheistic religions and membership in heaven is exclusive to each of these religions. The coexistence movement came up with the idea that all of these religions are right and that all of their members get into heaven. Unfortunately, that goes against the basic premise of these religions; so, it cannot be true. For example, in

Islam, if you are not a follower of Mohammed, you are an infidel and therefore you are barred from entrance into heaven. Quite honestly, the coexistence movement is an insult to the true believers of these major monotheistic, exclusive religions.

The last idea flows from the failure of the first three and the clear idea that heaven is God's domain and as such, He sets the rules and not us. If God sets the rules, how can we learn what they are?

This is why the idea of the Incarnation is so important in classic Christianity. The Incarnation is the idea that God is big, really big, and as such, He is very hard for us to grasp. Therefore, He decided to make it easier for us by coming down to earth Himself. He did not just send prophets who speak His word, He came Himself. Since He is so far beyond us in power, wisdom, justice, and mercy; to name a few; He decided to pour Himself into human form and live among us. This is the purpose of Jesus being born in Bethlehem about 2,000 years ago so that God could live among us and speak to us about who He is and show us how to live. Jesus did not only speak and live, but he died for us. Jesus made it clear that God's rules of heaven are clear and simple:

1. You must be perfect to live there. This solves the problems of #1 and #2 above.
2. You are not perfect now. This acknowledges the shortcomings of #2 and #3 above.

3. Not only are you not perfect, but you live in active rebellion against God and his rules, see Romans 1 again.
4. To get into a right relationship with Him, you must acknowledge your rebellious heart, place the penalty for your rebellion on Jesus on the cross, and then agree to take Him as the Lord of your life.
5. This puts you in a right relationship with God and He is then delighted to have you in His heaven forever.

This rule set is called the good news, the Gospel, and as such, it is available to everyone. However, you must be interested in living in God's place, under His rules, with Him as your personal Lord and Savior. If you are interested there is a helpful prayer at the end of this book.

Discussion Questions

1. How does the rule set given in the reading make sense for getting into heaven? How does it not make sense?

2. What would you say if others said that you were not good enough to get into heaven?

3. Has anyone ever called you arrogant for saying that your religion is the only way to get into heaven? How do you feel now that you see that it is not your religion, but God's rules that matter? What would you say to them?

If God Is Sovereign, What is Free Will?

There is a great deal of discussion around free will, both on the religious and scientific sides. On the scientific side, if we are indeed driven by the survival of the species using the survival of the fittest, perhaps all of our decisions are driven by these unconscious desires. On the religious side, if we all participate in the fall of the human species with the fall of Adam, do we have free will?

To better understand this discussion, we must first tackle what free will really means. We can all agree that we have intellect, will, and passion. Sometimes these are fully aligned, but perhaps more often we have internal conflicts. We might dissect this issue by thinking about the mind providing our intellectual ideas, and our heart driving us with passion. Our will is the mind choosing. The mind supplies the reason for our free will choice, our heart supplies the passion and the will is the bridge between the two.

We know that our choices are complex and dynamic and they sometimes change moment by moment. Take, for example, we have chosen to lose some weight. As we are reticent to exercise, we are going to eat less. We find that we can stick with this choice until we are presented with our favorite dessert. We then chose to eat the dessert, even though we had chosen to be on a diet just a few hours ago. In this example, we made a free will choice to eat the dessert because that was our strongest inclination at that moment in time.

Even though our choices have boundaries, we still have free will. For example, I know that I cannot jump 50 feet in the air to grab my favorite dessert off of a windowsill, but I still can get the dessert by climbing the stairs. The fact that there are insurmountable boundaries does not negate my free will. I may still be limited in what I can do, for example, I cannot jump to the moon, but I still can choose my strongest inclination at the time to do what I will. We can call this our natural ability.

The discussion gets more complicated when we consider our moral ability. Our moral choices are still driven by our minds, our wills, and our passions. The mind still supplies the reason for our free moral choice. We still make each moral choice based on our strongest inclination at the time. So, the real question is; "Can I choose to be perfect?"

Let's consider one subset of moral perfection, the choice to be totally selfless and not selfish. Can we choose to be totally unselfish? Real life would seem to indicate that we cannot choose to be totally unselfish, nor do we want to be totally unselfish. Why is that?

Darwin would say that our drive for the survival of the fittest would require us to always be looking out for ourselves and therefore selfishness is a strength to be encouraged. This would bind our moral will to always consider the need of our survival in our moral choices.

The Bible has a different take our this in that in the Garden of Eden Adam and Eve made a free moral choice to disobey God and in fact to compete with Him. God had made his creatures to have perfect free will, as long as they remained in the correct created order, subordinate to His love and authority. When they chose to rebel against His love and authority, they lost their ability to unselfishly chose. They showed that they desired to be selfish creatures and always be looking out for "number one."

So yes, we do have a free will. We can always choose the act that is our strongest inclination at the time. We also find that we most often choose based on our own selfish disposition. We seem to be stuck with this selfishness.

Perhaps these are two different ways to think about our inability to consistently make totally unselfish moral choices have some similarities between them. The main area where they differ is that God made a plan for His creatures to come back to Him in a loving relationship under His authority. He came up with a plan of redemption where we could agree to give up our selfishness and He would agree to indwell us to give us new hearts that could begin to make us into new people, unselfish people.

God is sovereign, He is ultimately in charge, but He still lets us choose the path that matches our strongest inclination. However, our choices are somehow bound by His sovereignty. An example of this can be found in the story of Joseph and his brothers. The brothers treated Joseph horribly and sold him off to slavers. Even though Joseph went through many years of slavery and imprisonment, he never lost his faith in God. God then allowed Joseph to miraculously interpret Pharaoh's dreams and Pharaoh appointed Joseph to be Prime Minster over all of Egypt to help deal with the coming famine. Joseph not only saved all of Egypt from the famine, but he also saved his brothers and all of Israel.

After Joseph's father died, there was a reconning time between Joseph and his brothers. The brothers were terrified that Joseph would punish them, perhaps even execute them, but Joseph only saw God's sovereign hand at work.

19 Joseph said to them, "Do not be afraid, for am I in the place of God? 20 But as for you, you meant evil against me; but God meant it for good, in order to bring it about as it is this day, to save many people alive. 21 Now therefore, do not be afraid; I will provide for you and your little ones." And he comforted them and spoke kindly to them. (Genesis 50:19-21)

Joseph saw how God had used the evil committed by his brothers for good. They acted out their free will in their jealous act of selling Joseph to slavers. Yet, somehow, God worked through their evil acts, committed freely out of their own jealousy.

He can be sovereign and work through our own sinful, free-will acts. Still, we need His help to make better choices with our free will. Our freedom seems to be mired in our own selfishness, and we cannot break out of that.

God says that cannot get there on our own, we need His help. He needs to help us with our free choices.

Discussion Questions

1. What do you think about your life choice so far? Did you freely choose them?

2. Have you chosen to be unselfish in the past? How did that work out?

3. Do you need God to help you to make some better life choices?

4. Are you free to make these choices? Do you want to make them? What is stopping you?

Blind Trust vs. Evidence-Based Faith

What is the difference between trust and faith? The definition of faith is trust. However, often we associate religious faith with blind faith. There is blind faith, but there is an even better evidence-based faith.

First, let's begin with trust in science. What exactly does that mean? It usually means that we have run a scientific hypothesis through the scientific method. We first start with an idea and then we do a set of clearly defined tests to attempt to verify or disprove the hypothesis. This works very well to verify that the acceleration of gravity is about 9.8 m/sec^2, but it does not work as well concerning the origin of the universe.

For the origin of the universe, things are more complicated. We can start with a hypothesis, like the steady-state model from about 50 years ago. We can then observe various objects in the sky and we observe that they generally move away at different speeds. Of course, we cannot directly observe the speed of any faraway galaxies, but we can infer their speed from the observed redshift. If indeed the science of the redshift is the same for objects close to us and those far away, then we can use the amount of the redshift to determine their speed.

Notice that a subtle trust or faith has snuck into the discussion. We trust that the science that determines the redshift is the same everywhere in the universe. But why should it be? Some of the faraway objects are believed to be from the first moments of the Big Bang when the laws of physics were not the same as they are today. The redshifted light is believed to be made billions of years ago. Is there any reason why the redshift must be the same 10 billion years ago? We trust that these laws are the same even though we have no way to scientifically verify that they are the same.

We trust that the laws of science have order and meaning to them, otherwise, we could not make any sense of the world around us. We could call this blind trust or perhaps reasonable trust, but it is trust that cannot be proven with direct observation.

Another simple example is Occam's Razor which goes something like this; *the simplest explanation is usually the best*. We believe this, but do we have any scientific basis to believe this? Has it been proven? No, it makes sense, so we take it on faith.

Much of Christianity is based on faith, that is trust, but it is an evidence-based faith. For example, after Jesus' resurrection from the dead, He appeared to many of His followers. They could see Him, touch Him, and talk with Him. However, one of His close followers named Thomas was not with the other followers. He did not believe their wild stories about the resurrection from the dead. He said;

"Unless I see in His hands the print of the nails, and put my finger into the print of the nails, and put my hand into His side, I will not believe." (John 20:25)

Thomas, the Doubter, was an early scientist. He wanted to see evidence that backed up their outstanding claims.

Eight days later Jesus visited his followers, including Thomas, and He offered for Thomas to touch His hands, feet, and His side. Thomas saw and believed.

Then He said to Thomas, "Reach your finger here, and look at My hands; and reach your hand here, and put it into My side. Do not be unbelieving, but believing." And Thomas answered and said to Him, "My Lord and my God!" (John 20:27-28)

He had an evidenced-based faith, and he left a record of that for our inspection and understanding. Even Einstein saw a place for faith in the investigation of life when he said; "I cannot imagine a scientist without that profound faith."

Discussion Questions

1. What would it mean to put blind trust aside and investigate the evidence-based claims that Jesus made?

2. As with any historical facts, how do we trust or verify them?

3. Can we trust things that have been recorded in the past? What makes a recorder reliable?

4. Have you had a seeing-is-believing moment in life? What was it like?

Why Do We See the Sky as Blue?

On a bright, clear day, we see the sky as blue. People have often wondered why the sky is blue and in general, scientists have done a good job explaining why the sky is blue. However, they tend to miss the second part of the question, why do we <u>see</u> the sky as blue?

Believe it or not, the blue sky has the fingerprints of an Intelligent Designer all over it.

We get our natural light from the sun; hence, sunlight. The sun radiates electromagnetic energy across a wide range of wavelengths; from radio waves with 10s of meters of wavelength to X-rays with wavelengths that are around a billionth of a meter.

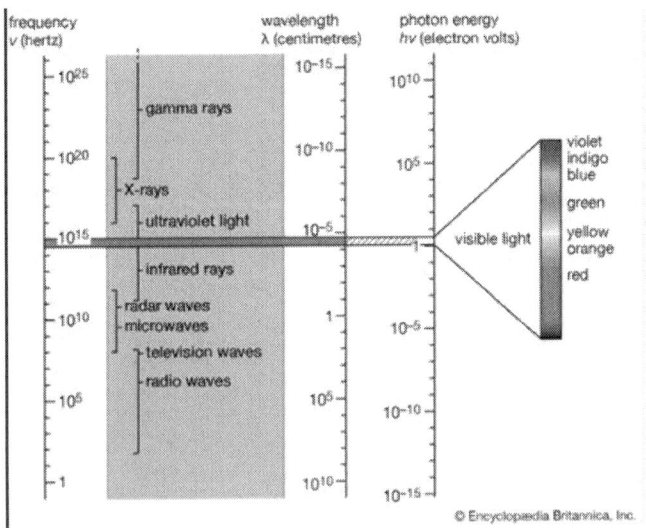

frequency v (hertz)		wavelength λ (centimetres)	photon energy hv (electron volts)	
10^{25}		10^{-15}	10^{10}	
	gamma rays			violet
10^{20}		10^{-10}	10^{5}	indigo blue
	X-rays			green
10^{15}	ultraviolet light	10^{-5}		yellow orange
	infrared rays		visible light	red
10^{10}	radar waves microwaves	1	10^{-5}	
	television waves			
	radio waves			
10^{5}		10^{5}	10^{-10}	
1		10^{10}	10^{-15}	

© Encyclopædia Britannica, Inc.

Somewhere in the middle of this electromagnetic spectrum is visible light which goes from 400 billionths of a meter for violet light to 750 billionths of a meter for red light.

Most of this radiated electromagnetic energy goes straight through the Earth's atmosphere. So, we only see it if we look straight at the sun (which is not a great idea as the sun is very bright and dangerous to our eyes). However, totally unrelated to the electromagnetic spectrum section of visible light, the Intelligent Designer filled the Earth's atmosphere with many gases; such as nitrogen and oxygen. These gaseous molecules are just the right size so that they only scatter some parts of the electromagnetic spectrum. The part that they scatter the most is of course blue light.

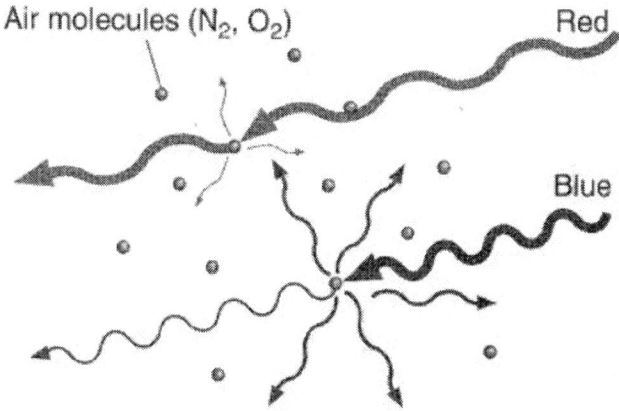

Air molecules (N_2, O_2)   Red

Blue

- U Oregon

110

This is why when we look up at the sky on a bright, summer day; we see the sky to be blue. The blue light from the sun is most strongly scattered by the atmospheric molecules so that no matter where in the sky we look, we see blue light.

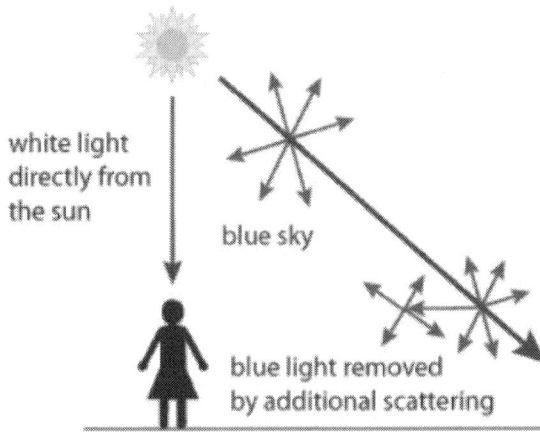

white light directly from the sun

blue sky

blue light removed by additional scattering

- Science Made Simple

Around sunset, the sun is lower in the sky, and the sunlight is going through more of the lower atmosphere which has many large dust particles. These large dust particles scatter red light more strongly. So, if everything is just right, we see a marvelous red and orange sunset.

This explains why the sky is blue, but it does not explain why we <u>see</u> a blue sky. Darwin's evolutionary theory postulates that everything evolves for the survival of the species, by favoring the survival of the fittest. However, Darwin was mystified by the human eye. It is such a complex design with about 90 million rods to help us see at night and 4.5 million cones to help us see color during the day. Darwin once mused on the origin of the eye; "To suppose that the eye, [with so many parts all working together] ... could have been formed by natural selection, seems, I freely confess, absurd in the highest degree."

Yet, the complexity of the eye is not the most fascinating aspect, but the fact that we see blue light so well is very fascinating. If you look out into a meadow, forest, or mountain scene, you will see predominately greens to browns. The animal that can distinguish objects in the green to brown spectrum should have the best chance for survival. If you look for plants and animals that have a significant amount of blue coloration, you will see very little. Most people can only count on one hand birds or animals that have a great deal of blue in their coloring.

So, why do we see blue so well? Surely it is not for our survival. Perhaps this is one way that the Intelligent Designer left His fingerprints on the world so that we would be sure to know of His creative work.

> *1 The heavens declare the glory of God;*
> *And the firmament shows His handiwork.*
> *2 Day unto day utters speech,*
> *And night unto night reveals knowledge.*
> *3 There is no speech nor language*
> *Where their voice is not heard.*
> *4 Their line has gone out through all the earth,*

*And their words to the end of the world.
(Psalm 19:1-4)*

From Darwin's survival of the fittest perspective, there is no reason why we should see the color blue so well, yet we do. Think about this for a minute and let it bring you joy.

Discussion Questions

1. How much more interesting is a color world compared to a black-and-white world?

2. Try an outdoor experiment and see how many blues you see, besides the sky. Could you do just as well if you could not see the color blue at all? What would you miss if you could not see the color blue?

3. Think of some famous works of art and describe how the artist used color and what colors they used.

4. What does the use of color tell us about a playful, joy-filled Creator?

Abortion Re-do. What Are the Latest Scientific Ideas on Abortion?

Sometimes issues and ideas get so entrenched in a society's paradigm that it is difficult to look at them with fresh eyes. We will attempt to do that with abortion. So, put all of your current ideas into a remote parking lot and try to look at this concept from a different perspective.

Abortion has been around for a long time in that it was a part of the Greek and Roman cultures. In the famous Oath of Hippocrates, he even mentions abortion; *"Neither will I administer a poison to anybody when asked to do so, nor will I suggest such a course. Similarly, I will not give a woman a pessary to cause abortion."* Hippocrates was setting forth prohibitions against euthanasia, murder by poison, and abortion. So, we have been debating abortion for a long time.

In the 1800s Charles Darwin wrote extensively on what we now call his Evolutionary Theory. He wrote that the primary purpose of any species is survival. The best way to accomplish this is for lots of members of the species to procreate. Given that there are lots of members of species, it is easier for the fittest to survive. One would think that Darwinists would not only be anti-abortion, but they would be ardent pro-life as the purpose of a species is to survive.

When we get to abortion language that is used today, it is not uncommon for language such as "the pregnancy just happened to the woman." It is an odd turn of phrase since we all know that pregnancies come from sex between a man and a woman. We also know that contraceptives are generally common and easy to obtain. We also know that a woman can only get pregnant at certain times of the month, so getting pregnant is sometimes hard work. Also, we would think that the couple would want their child to survive since almost all of us think that we are above average, and hence our prodigy would also be above average and hence good for the human race and society in general.

The second part of the discussion centers on the child. Watson, Crick, and Wilkins received the Nobel Prize for the molecular structure of DNA in 1962. So, we have known about unique DNA for quite a long time and we have known that the unborn child has unique DNA and hence is a unique individual. The child is not the same person as the mother or the father. We have also had a great scientific tool at our disposal since the 1950s, the ultrasound. Ultrasounds were developed and used in the late 50s. We have moved way past these initial 2-dimensional ultrasounds, to what we now call a 4-D ultrasound. The 4-D ultrasound can give us a real-time assessment of the child's face, breathing movements, swallowing, eye-blinking, and all sort of other indicators of the health and emotions of the child.

Science certainly tells us that the unborn child is a unique individual and can monitor the state of his or her health. We also know that there are many individuals in society that cannot fully take care of themselves. As a society we care for them, and in some cases feed them and take care of their physical needs because we can and we know that they are worth the effort. As a society, we view it as a good thing to take care of those who cannot take care of themselves.

Today, we often hear the cry for abortion that goes something like; "my body, my choice." It is a curious statement because we all know that we cannot do anything we want to or with our bodies. For example, just because I am a really good boxer and I enjoy it immensely, and I most enjoy hitting other people; that does not allow me to hit anyone whom I please. The counterargument would be that I cannot do it because it harms another person.

The same is true with alcohol consumption. While I can consume as much alcohol as I like, I cannot be drunk and drive a vehicle. Even though it is my body, and I have the right to consume as much alcohol as I like, I cannot use my body to drive a vehicle as again, I might harm another person.

The same is also true with drug overdoses. I am allowed to voluntarily give myself a lethal drug overdose. I might do it to experience this overdose level or I might do it because I am tired of life and I want to end it. If then, an emergency responder comes to my aid and saves me from a fatal drug overdose, do I then have the right to sue them because they violated my personal rights?

We can see that the discussion on abortion is quite complex. Oddly enough, science would strongly come on the side of saving the unborn baby; as it is a unique individual that may one day greatly help all of humanity. Darwin would agree with the idea of saving the baby. As a society, we generally side on the side of helping and saving children as they are the future of our society. No children equals no society.

To help understand the abortion issue with a new set of eyes, here is abortion by the numbers:

- Roughly 1 out of 100 women between 15 and 44 will have an abortion each year
- 95% will be done at an Abortion Clinic
- 60% of the women will be in their 20's
- 30% in their 30's
- 85% will be unmarried
- 30% will be Black, out of 14% of the population
- 50% will be below the Federal poverty level
- For 33% it will be their 2nd or 3rd abortion

The numbers tell us that many aborted babies come from a situation with young, unmarried women not practicing safe sex, in general, they are on the poor side of the socioeconomic spectrum, and for at least one-third, it will not be their first abortion.

In general, we think emotionally about the abortion issue. This leads to us often having conflicting views on abortion. For example:

"A third of Americans hold these seemingly conflicting views about the autonomy of pregnant women and the rights of the fetus at the same time, saying that both statements describe their views either extremely well, very well, or somewhat well. 'Life begins at conception AND the decision to have an abortion belongs solely to the woman'

The majority of abortion rights supporters say how long the woman has been pregnant should matter in determining the legality of abortion."

- Pew research on religion in 2022

One-third of us believe that life for the baby begins at the earliest possible moment, and yet even though the baby is alive, the baby has no right to live. Also, the father, who provided one-half of the DNA has no say in the decision to save the baby's life. It seems strange that we can hold these contradictory thoughts together in our collective minds. It would seem that both Hippocrates and Darwin would have a big problem with our current view on abortion.

Discussion Questions

1. What do you think about these seemly contradictory views of life beginning at conception and the woman having full rights on the abortion decision?

2. Why do we think about the scientific view of abortion being called a Basic Human Right or a Reproductive Right?

3. If the abortion issue came up for the first time in this time period, instead of in the 1970s, would there be a different scientific, social, or moral viewpoint?

4. How does this re-do discussion change your thinking, if at all? Should you do anything about this?

What Path to Take? How Can We Think About Hard Issues?

I t is often very hard to know what path to take in life. For example, we sometimes hear the question; "Should I get an abortion?" We know from a scientific perspective, that the answer would be "No", as the purpose of any species is to survive by creating more and better progeny. However, the choice can be much more difficult from an individual's perspective. If only we could see all future paths.

This is a time to reach out to the One who knows, God. The Bible speaks to this problem from several different perspectives.

> *23 The steps of a good man are ordered by the LORD,*
> *And He delights in his way.*
> *24 Though he fall, he shall not be utterly cast down;*
> *For the LORD upholds him with His hand.*
> *(Psalm 37:23-24)*

> *9 A man's heart plans his way,*
> *But the LORD directs his steps. (Proverbs 16:9)*

> *105 Your word is a lamp to my feet*
> *And a light to my path. (Psalm 119:105)*

The Bible speaks about a heavenly Father who is engaged in the lives of His children. He orders their steps, even though they often chose to take the wrong path. He upholds His children when they fall. He gives us His Word as a way to illumine the path ahead. However, we rarely take the time to ask Him what would be best for us. We can get a great deal of help by reading the Bible and talking to wise friends who can help us see both sides of a difficult issue.

On the subject of abortion, we may hear that we do not know where our lives or the child's life would be 20 years hence, but we can know for sure that if we abort, there will not be a path for the child.

Oddly enough, we hear of these same arguments in the US on the issue of undocumented immigrants. These are people who have come to the US to visit family, work temporarily, or for other reasons. As they are undocumented, that means that they cannot vote or pay income taxes. However, they can take full advantage of a free public education system and some healthcare systems.

There are often heated discussions concerning how many undocumented immigrants should any country allow. The US currently has more than 10 million undocumented immigrants. Many of them are taking advantage of the free public education system. Should they be allowed to do this? If so, how many for how long? Will some of them be the next Albert Einstein or Steve Jobs? How would we know?

Another complex topic today is climate change. We cannot even agree with the climate is changing in a bad way or not. We cannot agree on what to do, if anything. We often think that there are short-term solutions to long-term problems. Unfortunately, there are rarely short-term fixes for long-term messes.

We seem to have lost our ability to listen. Largely because of our addiction to smartphones and social media, we have lost our ability to talk to each other, face-to-face. And more importantly, we have lost the ability to listen, really listen to others. Perhaps it is time to learn to listen again, on several different levels.

First, we need to learn to listen to our friends, people who think like us. This should be easy to do, as they think like we do. Next, we need to learn to listen, really listen to others who think differently than we do. We need to really try to understand their viewpoint. A good way to do this is to listen for a bit and then repeat back to them their viewpoint, hopefully without sarcasm.

Next, we need to listen to the Elders of the community. In ancient times this was a common practice, to listen to the community Elders as they spoke with wisdom. Their wisdom was a knowledge that was tempered by life experiences. This wisdom only came with the many ups and downs in life that they experienced.

Most important, we need to learn to listen to God again. He cares deeply about us and the world that He created. We need to listen to Him through

His written Word. As we get to know Him better, we will gain His wisdom which would help us deal with the tough decisions in life. For He tells us

If any of you lacks wisdom, let him ask of God, who gives to all liberally and without reproach, and it will be given to him. (James 1:5)

We need to think seriously about the path that we want to be on. Perhaps it is time to ask for help for wisdom on these issues.

Discussion Questions

1. Why is it so hard to make hard decisions today?

2. If we are going to talk with our neighbors about difficult topics such as immigration or abortion, what do we need more of?
   a. Better facts and data?
   b. More listening and less shouting?
   c. Time spent learning about the other person's life story?

3. How can we better bring God's perspective into our discussion on heated and controversial subjects?

Fossil Formation Questions. A New Way of Thinking

We were all taught as kids that fossils take a long time to form. We picture a dinosaur that dies near an old river bed and falls down to the ground. Slowly, over many years, rock forms around the dinosaur, and years and years later his bones are captured in the sedimentary rock. However, there are a few things that are odd about this picture.

When an animal falls dead on the ground a huge neon light goes off that says "Free food, fresh meat here!" The sight and smell of this fresh meat would attract all kinds of scavengers. Scavengers are not known to be very polite eaters. They fight over their food. They rip it off of the bones. Often in the scuffling, the bones get widely scattered. Some of the bones are badly broken as the scavengers attempt to get the fresh marrow out of the bones. Near the end of the feast, the weakest scavengers come and pick through the bones. They may even carry the bones off to a safe haven to be eaten later. It would seem that the probability of finding dinosaur bones lying next to each other in the correct anatomical position would be astronomically small. It would seem that the only way the bones could be in the correct position is if the animal was buried very quickly like in a mudslide or an overflowing river bank.

Another thing that seems so odd is that dinosaurs are often found together, in groups. Again, why is this? Do we see piles of dead

126

animals or animal bones in the African safari today? No, generally not.

The standard methodology that we were taught as kids; time, chance, struggle, and death does not seem to fit the data.

In case you have not had a chance to visit a dinosaur burial site, here is an image from the Dinosaur National Monument in Colorado.

Do these bone positions fit with the model that we were taught? In light of the thoughts above, does this model make the most sense?

From this discussion above it is easy to see that as a society we often carry the ideas that we learned as children into adulthood. It seems strange that some of our childish ideas do not get corrected by the scientific community. One of the reasons for this is that there is no driving need to make the correction. There is no new scientific theory yet in place to replace the old idea, so the old idea is just left in place. Unfortunately, a second reason old ideas are not quickly replaced by new and better ideas is money. Funding for scientific research is often difficult to obtain and the committees that approve the funding are usually the old and staid members of the community. These members are reluctant to have some of the old ideas replaced, because many of these ideas are theirs.

This means that you should feel free to question any scientific idea, old or new. It just might be possible that there are weaknesses in the theory being presented and we just need someone to shine a light on the theory in a new way. After all, in Paul's letter to the Thessalonians he tells us *"Test all things; hold fast what is good."* (I Thessalonians 5:21)

Discussion Questions

1. How do the bones of a mostly complete dinosaur fit with the model that we were taught? In light of the thoughts above, does the rapid flooding model make more sense?

2. How can we go about rethinking scientific theories that we were thought as children?

3. How can you have a calm and loving discussion with your neighbors about your faith and science?

How Can We Best Think About Fossil Dating?

Fossils are had to date. The most common way to date a fossil or rock formation is by using the relative method. If a fossil in a rock layer has a different rock layer above it and a different rock layer below it, it is assumed that the fossil rock layer on top is younger and the layer on the bottom is older. This makes a lot of sense. However, it is much more difficult to determine the absolute age of a fossil or rock formation.

Absolute dating often starts with a discussion of carbon-14 dating, possibly because this is easy for most people to understand. Carbon exists in several isotopes, the two in question are carbon-12 and carbon-14. Carbon-12 is the more common, making up about 99% of the atmosphere, Carbon-12 is stable, so it does not change or decay. Carbon-14 is an isotope of carbon. It is radioactive, in that it undergoes beta decay and it has a half-life of 5,730 years. The half-live means that if you had 1 kg of carbon-14, after 5,730 years you would have about 0.5 kg of carbon-14. The tricky part of carbon dating is that carbon-14 is not very prevalent. The ratio of carbon-12 to carbon-14 is about 1/1,000,000,000,000.

All living creatures bring in carbon by eating or breathing and so they are always refreshing the ratio of carbon-14 to carbon-12 in their bodies. When they die, they stop refreshing the ratio of carbon-14 to carbon-12 and so as the carbon-14 decays the ratio changes a little bit each year. One tricky assumption is that over the last 10,000 to 40,000 years the ratio of carbon-14 to carbon-12 in the biosphere has been exactly the same, to one part in 1,000,000,000,000. As it is a look back in time, this is difficult to prove. Rather, it is a scientific assumption to be believed to be true.

Carbon-14 dating is good for dating things that were once living and have been around for a few thousand years to about 40,000 years (6 or 7 half-lives). Here is a graphic explanation of half-live decay.

Radioactive Decay

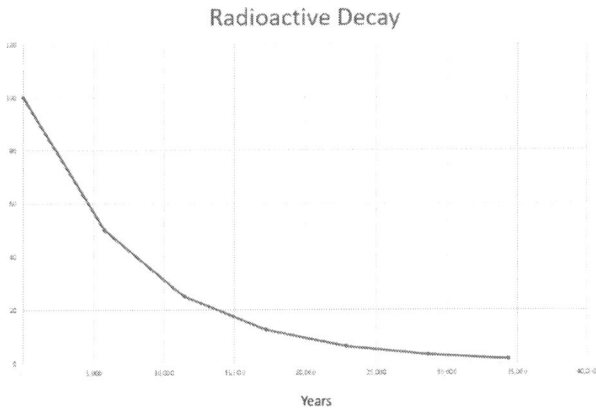

Years

Carbon-14 dating is not useful for things that are projected to be 500 M years old. The reason for this is that all of the carbon-14 in the now-dead organism would have all decayed away. There would not be any carbon-14 left.

To date objects that are millions of years old, it is helpful to have prevalent elements that are radioactive with a half-life of a few hundred million years. Unfortunately, there are very few elements that fit these parameters, prevalent and have a good half-life. The closet is uranium. It is radioactive and it is somewhat prevalent. Uranium has several isotopes of interest, U-238, and U-235. Uranium-235 has a half-life of about 700 million years; however, unfortunately, it is not very prevalent. It makes up about 0.7% of uranium ore. Uranium-238 is much more prevalent making about 99.4% of the uranium ore. Unfortunately, U-238 has a half-life of 4.5 billion years. Therefore, to measure a fossil that is to be about 540 million years old, from the Cambrian period, only 0.13% of the uranium-238 would have decayed. However, uranium-235 would work from a half-life perspective (700 million years), it is just not very prevalent.

Again, using uranium isotopes to measure the age of fossils that are thought to be hundreds of millions of years old takes very sophisticated equipment and the assumption that the ratio of U-238 and U-235 has not changed over millions of years, while both of the isotopes are decaying at their own rates.

To date very old fossils, there are lots of assumptions to be taken on scientific faith. This is why the relative method is so common. Once a rock layer can be identified (named) as being from a certain time period, it is an obvious assumption that all of the fossils in that rock layer are from that time period. But what would happen if the relative method was flawed?

The absolute methods using radioactive decay also have some key assumptions, not proven facts, that undergird them. What would happen if some of these assumptions were flawed?

Hopefully, you can see from this discussion that the science behind dating objects that are reported to be very old can be quite complicated. So, when you hear about something being dated by using the relative method, feel free to ask deeper questions about the dating method. It is okay to ask "How do you know?"

Discussion Questions

1. There are lots of assumptions concerning science and time. As hard as we try, some of them may be wrong. What would happen if the relative method for fossil dating was flawed?

2. What is the best way to question scientific assumptions that you hear about given that you are not an expert in this field of study?

3. Another unproven statement is Occam's Razor "that this simplest explanation is often the best." While this may be helpful most of the time, it could lead us out of God's path for us unless we look at the problem differently. Can you describe a situation like this?

The Dead Sea Scrolls and Carbon Dating. Why Is This Important?

Ancient documents do not last forever, yet historians take great pains to try to dig up the oldest version of any ancient historical document so that they can learn more and validate other later documents. For example; Julius Caesar wrote a chronicle of his military conquests entitled *The Gallic Wars*. This document is used by many historians to chronicle the Roman Empire, its expansion, and life in general during those times. The earliest copy that exists today is from nine hundred years later, in the eighth century AD. We use this copy because it is the best copy that we have and we believe that it is a reliable copy of the original document.

People often wonder about the Bible. It was written thousands of years ago, so how do we know that what we have today is a reliable copy of the original text?

In 1947, a shepherd boy was watching his sheep and goats in the area of the Dead Sea. One of his goats had wandered off, up the cliffs, in amongst some caves. Being generally curious, the boy wandered deeper into one cave and he discovered a bunch of old clay pots. He opened one of the pots and saw that it contained what appeared to be an ancient scroll.

In ancient times, it was easier to write on scrolls instead of books for several reasons. The parchment, that is animal skins, did not need to be cut to a uniform size. A scroll did not need a binding material. A scroll did not need a cover, it was just wrapped up, covering itself.

These particular scrolls were very well preserved for several reasons. They were in a very arid region, so they did not have moisture decay. The writing material was sheepskin so they did not deteriorate as paper would. The writing was done with soot and not ink. Soot, or ash from a fire, is generally inert to interactions with the atmosphere.

It was eventually determined that they contained parts from thirty-seven of the thirty-nine books of the Jewish Old Testament. Some of the scrolls were from the fourth century BC, meaning they were only a few hundred years removed from the original text.

These documents caused a great debate between the religious, historical, and scientific communities. Everyone wondered how they could verify that these documents were as old as the religious community said they were. This is where science came into the picture to work alongside the religious community.

Finding purported old documents is one thing, but dating them is quite another. As it turns out, this is a perfect application for carbon dating. For carbon dating, the object must have been alive at one time and therefore ingesting carbon. This would be true for both the sheepskin parchment and the writing soot. Carbon dating works well for things that are a few thousand years old, as the half-life of Carbon-14 is 5,730 years. This means that every 5,730 years half the existing Carbon-14 would decay away. If these documents were fake, that is a few hundred years old, the Carbon-14 ratio would be way off. If there were around 2,000 to 3,000 years old, the Carbon-14 decay would be about half of one half-life. After exhaustive and detailed carbon-14 dating tests, these documents were reported to be a little over 2,000 years old. They were written very close to the time of the original text.

Can you imagine these last verses from the Book of Malachi from the almost original text?

4 "Remember the Law of Moses, My servant,
Which I commanded him in Horeb for all Israel,
With the statutes and judgments.
5 Behold, I will send you Elijah the prophet
Before the coming of the great and dreadful day of the LORD. (Malachi 4:4-5)

Perhaps the most surprising discovery was that the texts were virtually identical to the modern text. This meant that over hundreds of years, the Jewish scribes faithfully copy the text for the next generation. Jewish scribes were well trained to make exact copies of any given text and with this discovery, the work of the old scribes was validated.

The Dead Sea Scrolls are a wonderful example of where science and faith come together. As it turns out, the concurrence of science and faith is not all that uncommon. Can you think of some other examples? Perhaps this inspires you to investigate some other areas of science and faith concurrence.

Discussion Questions

1. Think about all of the pieces of life that had to come together for the finding and dating of the Dead Sea Scrolls. First, someone had to faithfully copy the Old Testament documents. They had to use parchment and soot and not paper and ink. They had to store them in clay jars. They had to seal the jars very well... what other parts of this story can you imagine? (We call this seeing the fingerprints of God).

2. How important is it to you that the Bible you are reading today is the same text as thousands of years ago? Why or why not?

What Does God Think About Technology? Is It Good or Bad?

What does God think about technology? Well, He probably likes it, as He invented it. Early in the Bible, three of Cain's descendants are credited with the technology of animal husbandry, musical instruments, and bronze and iron metalwork (Genesis 4:20-22). These are three important parts of any civilized community. Food, milk, and clothing from sheep, goats, and cows. Music to build community and excite the passions of the heart. Bronze and iron to build tools, machines, and of course, instruments of war.

God probably views technology like He views gravity. Gravity is a key to holding the world together as it is key to making water flow from cool, clear, and high mountain lakes downhill to the community below. Technology is much the same way; it is neither good nor bad on its own; it is all about how mankind uses it. After all, gravity, pushing water downhill, makes the water wheel work, which was the technology that drove much of our early civilization.

In the book of the prophet Isaiah, he talks about the blacksmith. The blacksmith was one of the community's most important members, making everything from horseshoes to kitchen tools.

"Behold, I have created the blacksmith
Who blows the coals in the fire,
Who brings forth an instrument for his
work;

And I have created the spoiler to destroy.
(Isaiah 54:16)

God acknowledges that He made the blacksmith and gave him his unique gifts and talents. The blacksmith was the one who knew how to mine the right kind of ore. He knew how to build a fire hot enough using a bellows system. He knew how to heat the ore and then pound it into the correct shape for its intended use. He could make himself a new set of longer tongs or an instrument of war for the spoiler (destroyer).

Think of all of the uses of metalwork in today's world. Think about how we use steel to reinforce our concrete, to give our bridges strength, and to allow our buildings to grow tall. Think about how we use plastics today. They are used in drinking straws in a restaurant and IV tubes in a hospital. Plastics are used to keep our food fresh as well as for our garbage cans.

How about nuclear energy? We went from exploding two atomic bombs to generating about 20% of the electrical power in the United States with nuclear power plants in just about fifty years.

Can we even envision a world without technological advances in communication? Can we imagine going back to a world with no Internet, no mobile phone, and no streaming video?

Where will technology take us over the next one hundred years? Will it take us to live on the Moon and Mars? Will it remove all disease and hunger? Will it make us better people?

It is easy to see that technology itself will not give us new products or solve all our problems. Technology is driven by people. Who will decide how technology is used in the future? Will we be able to reign in our evil desires? Will technology take us to places that are outside of God's sovereignty?

Discussion Questions

1. Can we even envision a world without technological advances in communication? Can we imagine going back to a world with no Internet, no mobile phone, and no streaming video? What would it be like to go back in time to this world?

2. Where will technology take us over the next one hundred years? Will it take us to live on the Moon and Mars? Will it remove all disease and hunger? Will it make us better people? What do you think should be our highest priority?

3. It is easy to see that technology itself will not give us new products or solve all our problems. Technology is driven by people. Who will decide how technology is used in the future? Will we be able to reign in our evil desires? How can we put reigns on new technology?

4. Will technology take us to places that are outside of God's sovereignty? Why or why not?

Who Made the Nails? What Happens When Technology Goes Wrong?

Many people are surprised when they hear that God invented technology. In the early chapters of Genesis, God talks about creation, people, and technology. "And as for Zillah, she also bore Tubal-Cain, as an instructor of every craftsman in bronze and iron" (Genesis 4:22). Metalwork was as important in the ancient world as it is today. In the ancient world all the way into the industrial age; the metalworker, blacksmith, and ironworker were very important members of society.

For thousands of years, the blacksmith was a revered member of society. He was responsible for making many of the tools of the age. He was responsible for shoeing the horses, making the wagon wheels, and making the bridles. The local economy barely functioned without a good blacksmith. If a small community did not have a blacksmith of their own, members of that community had to travel to another community that had a blacksmith. This was a big problem in ancient Israel for they had no blacksmiths.

19 Now there was no blacksmith to be found throughout all the land of Israel, for the Philistines said, "Lest the Hebrews make swords or spears." 20 But all the Israelites would go down to the Philistines to sharpen each man's plowshare, his mattock, his ax, and his sickle... (I Samuel 13:19-20)

Around 1100 BC, the Philistines kept an economic and military advantage over the ancient Israelites with their metalworking technology. It was not until much later that the Israelites got skilled in metalworking. By 700 BC we know that the Israelites had their own blacksmiths, as the prophet Isaiah talks about God's role in bringing this technology forward.

"Behold, I have created the blacksmith
Who blows the coals in the fire,
Who brings forth an instrument for his work;
And I have created the spoiler [destroyer] to destroy. (Isaiah 54:16)

By the time we get to the time of Jesus, the Jews had a very strong love/hate relationship with the Romans. The Jews hated the oppression by the Roman army, government, and worship system. However, the Jews greatly benefited from Roman technology. They had free use of the wonderful system of roadways. They had access to clean water from the Roman aqueduct system. There was also a great system of free trade.

As such, the Jewish craftsmen flourished. They had great fishermen, shepherds, and even their own blacksmiths. Does access to great technology ever go wrong?

Image a skilled blacksmith in Jesus' day, whom we will call Samuel. He was a very talented blacksmith and he was beginning to be intrigued by the traveling rabbi, Jesus. Samuel had heard Jesus talking about being a peacemaker and turning the other cheek. He had heard about loving others. He had been contemplating the Golden Rule;

"Whatever you want men to do to you, do also to them. (Matthew 7:12)

Then tragedy struck and Jesus was brought before the Sanhedrin and Pilate. Even though Pilate could find no wrongdoing done by Jesus, he sentenced Him to crucifixion. Samuel followed the crowd to Golgotha, the place of crucifixion outside of the city. Samuel watched as Jesus was forced to carry His own cross up the hill. Then, much to Samuel's horror, he saw the Roman soldiers nailing Jesus to the cross with spikes that he made. Samuel recognized the unique head to the spike that was Samuel's signature on his work. Samuel collapsed in despair as he watched his technology being used for absolute evil.

Discussion Questions

1. Have you seen your technology being used for evil? How did you react?

2. What should we do in these situations where we see technology being used for evil?

3. How can we keep technology on the right track and not be used for evil?

Technology That is Good for the Community

I t is hard to define good or bad technology. In general, technology is neutral and it all comes around to how it is used.

Take, for example, nuclear energy. Nuclear power plants can produce electricity for a very long time without polluting the atmosphere with carbon dioxide and other by-products that come from coal-fired power plants. However, nuclear power plants are not totally clean as they have their own problem of disposing of spent nuclear fuel, which lasts a really long time. Of course, there can be horrible disasters, such as what happened in Chernobyl, Russia. Yet, almost 20% of the electrical power in the US is made from nuclear power plants.

When the Apple iPhone was launched in 2007, it was not the first smartphone. It was not the first device that played music, took photos, or had a web browser. However, it was the first device that did all of these things smoothly and simply. Was the iPhone great technology? No question. However, is smartphone technology all for good? Given the rise of loneliness among young adults, its goodness could be debated.

How could we better determine if early new technology is good for us and how can we put boundaries around its use?

The Amish people are viewed to be anti-technology, but that is not totally true. There are different uses of technology in different communities. But, many of them use the same test for new technology. They will bring a new technology into the community for use by just a few members. These members will use the technology for a limited time, say a few months. At the end of this time, the entire community assembles to discuss the merits of the new technology, with a particular focus on the benefit for the community, not the individual. This focus on the entire community is a different approach than most Western, technological societies.

An example of the Amish approach is the use of gasoline tractors by some Amish and Mennonites. They decided that the tractor was a useful piece of farm equipment. The tractor could plow, harvest and haul more effectively than a pair of horses. However, the Amish did not want the tractor used as transportation between communities, especially on asphalt roads. Therefore, they replaced the rubber tires with steel tires. The steel tires work well in the fields, but they do not work well on asphalt roads. On asphalt, they produce a very uncomfortable ride between communities. However, the tractor provides a great benefit to the community in terms of planting and harvesting. However, as a method of transportation between communities, it is a poor substitute for the horse and buggy. The buggy can carry many more people. It does not use expensive gasoline for fuel. It does not produce air pollution, and it does allow for community discussion during the journey.

Perhaps the Amish thought that Matthew expected the community to gather together face-to-face and not electronically or on social media:

> 19 *"Again I say to you that if two of you agree on earth concerning anything that they ask, it will be done for them by My Father in heaven.* 20 *For where two or three are gathered together in My name, I am there in the midst of them." (Matthew 18:19-20)*

Much of the time today, the technology discussion is focused on the benefit for the individual. Perhaps we all would be better off if we thought about technology beyond ourselves, beyond making money, and more about building community, when two or three of us gather together.

Photo credit: Reba Tyrrell

Discussion Questions

1. What do you think about this community view for technology? Are there any drawbacks to this community-view approach?

2. Can you think about how smartphone technology could be used for community building?

3. What drawback would there be to limiting the technology to a community-focus only?

4. What would it take for you to give up your personal smartphone?

Dominion Over the Creation. How Are We Doing?

26 Then God said, "Let Us make man in Our image, according to Our likeness; let them have dominion over the fish of the sea, over the birds of the air, and over the cattle, over all the earth and over every creeping thing that creeps on the earth." *(Genesis 1:26)*

Genesis 1:26 is a very strong and convicting message about the Creation and our role in it. First, it says that humankind is made in God's image. Part of what that means is that we have will, emotions, passion, thought, creativity, and the ability to get things done. This passage continues to say that we are to have dominion over the rest of the Creation. The Hebrew word, *radah,* is a complex word that means to rule over, reign, subjugate, or to have dominion. It is often further expanded to mean to be a caretaker or a steward. We are to have dominion over all of the rest of the Creation for the good of the Creation, for our own good, and to bring glory to the Creator. All in all, we have done a very poor job of being caretakers of the Creation.

One horrifying example of our poor stewardship is the Great Pacific Garbage Patch. As with most of our stories, it started out all good. Over a hundred years ago, we discovered oil. Besides all of its transportation uses, we discovered that we could use it to make all kinds of plastics. In many cases, plastic was a lifesaver because it could be used to store and transport clean water. In many parts of the world, without clean water, we die. Plastic bottles could provide clean water to a parched world. However, plastic bottles seem to have gone too far in that in the US alone about 500 billion plastic bottles are used every year.

We found that plastic could make lightweight containers that last a very long time. This was very good until we got tired of reusing and recycling the plastic containers, and we just threw them away. Much of our modern view of dominion is that if we have thrown it away and if it is out of our mind, then it is out of our life. Unfortunately for plastic, another of its annoying properties is that it floats. So, being thrown away means that it will eventually make its way to the ocean. Once it hits the ocean, the plastic will float with the currents and wind.

Plastic will float for a long time in the ocean and it will eventually make its way to one of the gyre regions. These regions are a confluence of several different ocean currents, and they tend to make a vortex that captures the plastic. Once the plastic makes its way to a gyre, it gets stuck there as there are no currents to push it anywhere else. As the plastic floats in the ocean waters for a long time, it will continue to collect in these gyre regions and just keep piling up. The plastic will eventually be broken into smaller pieces of plastic by the Sun, but it will never go away.

-    The Great Garbage Patch

The Great Pacific Garbage Patch was first discovered around 1990, and even at that time, it was huge. Unfortunately, it is growing an order of magnitude (ten times) every ten years, in 2020 it was estimated to be twice the size of the state of Texas. It is now so big that if 100 ships worked to clean it up for an entire year, they could clean up only about 1% of the Great Patch.

As the waste plastic comes from many nations and it is in the middle of the ocean, none of our nations are very interested in cleaning up the Patch. It is someone else's problem. It will remain someone else's problem until we realize that we are choking out many of the sea animals, and then it might be too late.

The Creation is a big place. The oceans are huge. That is why our dominion is a big job. It is not just dominion over our backyard, our community, and our natural resources, but it is over all of the created order.

Discussion Questions

1. What can we do to begin to turn back to our original creation task to have dominion over all of the Creation?

2. How can we work together on this? Or, is it too late?

3. What is the best way for you to work on environmental issues and have it be a solid Christian witness?

Why are Utopias so Hard?

Since the beginning of time, we have been trying to figure out how to live in a Utopian society. No matter how hard we try, Utopian experiments always seem to fall short of their objective. Why is that?

One of the main reasons for Utopian failure is food. We all need food to survive. In general, Utopian societies strive to be self-sufficient, so they do not want to depend on outsiders for survival and that means food. Food takes good soil, lots of water, and a fair amount of sunshine. Most importantly, the growing of food takes work and lots of it.

In any society, not everyone likes to work the same amount and in the same way. Not everyone is able to produce the same amount of output at any given task. Some of us are much better at some tasks than others. While it is important to have painters and poets in any given society, if the society is fairly small, everyone will have to do some of the work to grow food. Growing food is generally hard work! In some Utopian societies, hard physical labor is not highly valued. If hard work is not valued, these societies are destined to fail for a lack of food.

All societies need some form of Government. While anarchies have been attempted, they rarely succeed long-term. For much the same reasoning as above. There are tasks that few of us like or want to do, such as taking out the garbage, but it must be done. Without some structure, some governments, and societies collapse under the weight of their own garbage, both figuratively and literally. However, not all governments work. For a government to exert its will for the good of the people, it needs both power and money. Unfortunately, the old adage is usually true; "power corrupts and absolute power corrupts absolutely." Most societies cannot find the right balance of power and accountability to survive long-term, for those in power rarely want to relinquish their power. The utopian attempt fails because in one way or another those at the bottom of the power spectrum get tired of being on the bottom and they revolt. Those at the top will do everything in their power to stay at the top. Through this conflict, society fails.

Surprisingly another area where Uptonian societies fail is in the care of children. While everyone agrees that the care of children is important, they cannot agree on how to do it. Mothers tend to have a much stronger bond with their own children than they do with their annoying neighbor's children. So, with the idea that it takes a village to raise a child, distributed childcare becomes the best way to raise the children. Unfortunately, with distributed childcare, the care ends up being uneven. Every patent tends to give a little more attention to their own children. This uneven care allows all aspects of the natural personalities of young children to blossom. Some of the aspects of their early personalities are that children as selfish, demanding, needy, and not as obedient as their parents would like. Without great childcare and a focus on raising the next generation, the Utopian society fails in one generation.

Lastly, Utopian societies have difficulty with the sense of community and families. They sometimes swing too far to one side or the other. For example, consider where totally open marriages are encouraged. This often leads to the exportation of women and a strong feeling of loneliness. Loneliness can also occur if society mandates that everyone must get along. This does not allow individuals to share their difficulties and they fall into their own internal darkness of depression. Some Utopian societies struggle with their own purity and the question of; "Whom do we let in?" If they let everyone in, then some "bad" people can come in and corrupt their society. If they are too restrictive, they do not get a good enough mix of personalities and skill sets. Of course, they struggle with the question of who gets to decide who is allowed into their new society. Not everyone can agree on this. Fundamentally they cannot decide on the definition of the family and how to distinguish family from the overall community.

These are just some of the struggles that Utopian societies struggle with. It is interesting to see that these issues are dealt with early on in Genesis. God states that we are all made in His image and therefore He expects us to use our intellect, our wisdom, our wills, and our creativity.

²⁷ So God created man in His own image; in the image of God He created him; male

*and female He created them. ²⁸ Then God
blessed them, and God said to them, "Be
fruitful and multiply; fill the earth
and subdue it; have dominion over the fish
of the sea, over the birds of the air, and
over every living thing that moves on the
earth." (Genesis 1:27-28)*

We are also all supposed to be engaged in
purposeful activities, that is work, that entails filling
the earth, subduing it, and caring for it (Genesis
1:28). Even after the Fall, mankind was still to be
engaged in growing food, but it was just going to be
much harder and we would have to work by the
sweat of our faces.

*In the sweat of your face you shall eat
bread
Till you return to the ground,
For out of it you were taken;
For dust you are,
And to dust you shall return." (Genesis
3:19)*

From a governmental perspective, we are
created male and female and the differences are
celebrated. While males and females are different,
they are created to be mutual helpmates.

*And the LORD God said, "It is not good that
man should be alone; I will make him a
helper comparable to him." (Genesis 2:18)*

We are to work together, recognizing each other's strengths and weaknesses and never lording power over others. We are to acknowledge God as the source of all authority and we are to love and worship Him.

We are to be in a committed relationship where we bond with one another and we share of ourselves, without shame.

And they were both naked, the man and his wife, and were not ashamed. (Genesis 2:25)

From this basic family structure, all other relationships are to flow.

Discussion Questions

1. It seems like Genesis has a great deal to say about how we are to relate to each other and hence, how societies should work. What do you think about this?

2. Do you think that you could start a utopian society and make it work? Why or why not?

3. How would you handle these four main areas?
   - Food
   - Government
   - Family Life
   - Community Life

4. What you say to your best friends if they said that wanted you to join them in starting a Utopian society?

Green Transportation. Are We Close to Achieving This?

⁴ Joseph also went up from Galilee, out of the city of Nazareth, into Judea, to the city of David, which is called Bethlehem, because he was of the house and lineage of David, ⁵ to be registered with Mary, his betrothed wife, who was with child. ⁶ So it was, that while they were there, the days were completed for her to be delivered. (Luke 2:4-6)

In much of the Bible, the primary form of transportation was by foot. There were times that camels, donkeys, or chariots were used; but for most of the common folk, if you wanted to get somewhere, you walked.

In the case of Joseph and his very pregnant wife; they walked and rode a donkey for the 90-mile journey from Nazareth to Bethlehem.

Transportation changed very little for almost 1800 years, and then oil was discovered in Pennsylvania. It did not take too long for the scientists of the day to discover the many uses of this petroleum that came out of the ground. One of the many uses was to fuel transportation. This discovery had a major impact on society.

With petroleum-fueled transportation, people no longer needed to live very close to farms. Food could be trucked over many miles to bring it to the people. This gave birth to cities as well as a population explosion.

In Jesus' time, there were around 200 million people in the entire world. This is much less than the population of just the United States today. With 200 million people mostly walking for their entire lives, transportation pollution was not a big deal.

The global population stayed relatively constant until around the 1800s when the industrial revolution brought mobility to daily life and an explosion of activity and people. By the 1850s we passed the 1.2 billion population mark and by the 1900s the 1.6 billion mark. In 1950, we were at the 2.5 billion people mark. Since then, with the passing of every 15 years or so, we add another billion people to our global village and we are now surpassing 7.7 billion people.

Many of us need many goods shipped to our nations, our communities, and our homes. Almost all of this transportation is petroleum based. All of this transportation generates about 25% of our greenhouse gases. So why do we not just switch over to all-electric vehicles?

As with much of life, it is complicated. In the United States, there is a wonderful distribution infrastructure for gasoline. In just a few minutes, a vehicle can be filled with enough gasoline to go more than 300 miles. There are over 1,000,000 gasoline pumps throughout the US. While there are only about 40,000 electric charging stations. For electric vehicles, it takes 15 to 30 minutes to charge up at most of these stations. For impatient, on-the-go Americans this is too long of a time to have to wait to be convenient. Charging at home, overnight, is much more convenient; yet this only works well for those who live in single-family homes. For the 35% of Americans who rent apartments or live in condominiums, charging overnight is not a very good option. Unfortunately, it might take a long time to get enough charging stations, in the right places to be convenient for busy Americans.

The next problem is generating electricity. It does not do any good to generate electricity by burning coal as it just moves the greenhouse gas generation problem to a different part of the transportation cycle. Solar and wind are great examples of green electricity generation. However, good sunlight and good wind are not uniformly available everywhere in the US. Most of the northeastern cities like New York, Boston, Washington DC, Pittsburgh, and Chicago to name a few have poor sunlight throughout the year. The electricity would have to be generated a long way away and transported by high-voltage lines. These electricity transmission lines have electrical losses when transporting electricity over great distances. The other problem with sunlight and wind is that they are not available 24 hours a day. Therefore, an entirely new nationwide battery storage system would need to be developed.

And yet another problem is that almost all electrical systems are designed for moving the electricity one way, from the generated source point to the point of usage. For example, the electricity would go from the wind farm to the consumer's home. If the consumer was to have a great deal of electrical energy, say from solar panels on the roof, there is no way for the consumer to pass this electrical "up" to the electric company. To have the electricity go both ways, the electrical system would need to be significantly upgraded, and this would take a great deal of time and money.

All of these problems are solvable, but they take time and effort. Perhaps we need to take a lesson from Joseph who was sold to the Ishmaelites when he was 17 years old. He did not get out of the Egyptian prison until he was 30 years old. He had to wait 13 years before he could begin to help the Egyptians with their impending famine. The famine preparation took 7 years and the famine lasted another 7 years. Perhaps these stories are there to help us understand that some problems take a long time to solve, but they are all solved by moving forward one step at a time.

Discussion Questions

1. Which steps to solve the green transportation problems would you recommend that we take first?

2. How should a society prioritize these steps?

3. What geographies should we focus on first?

4. Read Genesis 41 with particular attention to how Joseph went about solving a very big problem. Are there any lessons in this story for us today?

Electric Vehicles – The Good and the Bad

E lectric vehicles (EVs) are all the rage now. Some say that they will save the world that we are all slowly destroying. While there are some good things about EVs, they are not all good. Let's look at some of the pluses and minuses.

The most obvious advantage of any electric vehicle is that they do not have any exhaust gases. This is a big advantage in any large city where air pollution is getting worse every year, largely due to the pollution from vehicles. The biggest problem with an internal combustion engine (ICE) vehicle is the carbon dioxide, carbon monoxide, and nitrous oxides that come out of the tailpipe.

A second benefit of electric vehicles is that they have a huge DC battery. In the early 2000s, a typical Tesla battery was about 110 kWh. As the typical American home uses almost 900 kWh per month (30 kWh per day), a battery of this size could power a home for several days, or perhaps a week with proper energy conservation.

For many, the biggest benefit of an EV is that they are fun to drive. They have instant acceleration as the DC current goes straight to the wheels. The torque that is generated makes for an exciting drive. They also have a low center of gravity due to the weight of the battery pack, so they feel like they handle well and they are hard to flip over.

There is no question that EVs are the way of the future; however, as Roy Amara said in 1960, "We overestimate the impact of technology in the short-term and underestimate the effect in the long run." EVs today have been given a great deal of hype and they are having trouble living up to it.

One of the drawbacks of electric vehicles is that they are more expensive than internal combustion engine vehicles. The average price of a plug-in electric car in 2022 was about $65,000, compared to the average new ICE car price of around $48,000. This almost $20,000 difference is hard for many Americans to absorb.

A second problem with an EV is the battery pack. They are not as green as everyone would hope. The manufacturing of an EV, especially the battery pack, is quite harmful to the environment. The current lithium battery technology has a huge amount of very toxic waste associated with the mining process. For example; it takes about 2,500 gallons of water, or 20,000 pounds of water, to make 1 pound of lithium. Also, it takes a lot of heavy diesel-powered, exhaust-spewing machines to mine the rare-earth materials used to make up the battery back. Many of these materials come from China, where green manufacturing processes are often shunned to reduce costs. The assembled battery pack is also quite heavy, weighing around 1,200 pounds. This increases the total weight of the car from around 3,5000 for a typical Honda Accord, to about 4,500 pounds for a typical Tesla. Obviously moving a heavier vehicle wastes more energy in motion.

Charging the EV is also a problem today. There are currently three charging situations; home, work, or a public station.

The main problem with public charging stations is that there are just not enough available today. While this will be resolved over time, it will take a great deal of time and money. In 2000, there were about 100,000 electric charging outlets, public and private, compared to over 1,000,000 gasoline pumps. This factor of ten difference will take a long time to overcome. Another problem with public charging stations is keeping them in good repair. They are sometimes accidentally damaged or at other times maliciously vandalized. For the public stations, the question is always; *Who will be responsible for keeping them in good repair?*

Many people view the problem to be resolved with the idea of charging stations at home. If everyone can start their day with the EV fully charged, public charging stations would be rarely needed. Unfortunately, the numbers in the United States just don't work out that well. There are about 43 M households that rent in the US. There is another 15 M who live in multi-dwelling units such as a condominium, townhouse, or similar structures. This means that about 58 M households will not have easy access to chargers at home. Even with single-family dwellings, another 44 M homes do not have a garage or a carport for a convenient charging location. If we assume half (22 M) do not have an easy solution to this charging problem, that means a total of about 80 M (about 60%) will not have a charger at home.

The weather can also be a problem for electric vehicles in general. Batteries do not, in general, do well with temperature extremes. They lose power capability at both very low temperatures (cold winters) and very high temperatures (hot summers). Therefore, they need some kind of temperature control system to protect the battery pack, which uses energy that could have otherwise been used for driving.

Another hope for electrical vehicles is for the EV to feed electrical energy back into the power grid during peak usage times. This still has a long way to go for several reasons. The first is that the power grid in the US is not designed as a two-way transmission network. It is designed to send electricity to your home or business and not the other way around. It will be a massive undertaking to make the power grid a two-way grid. The other problem is that the EV runs on direct current (DC) and not alternating current (AC) like your home. This means an expensive DC-to-AC converter is required to feed power back into the grid.

Perhaps the way forward is to have a better mix of plug-in electric hybrid vehicles (PEHV). The PEHV has a much smaller battery pack that is good for the typical commute distance of 30 or 40 miles. If the PEHV needs more electrical power, it gets it from a small, efficient gasoline engine in the vehicle. Because the battery pack is so much smaller, eight PEHV battery packs can be made for every one EV. This eight-to-one difference has a big impact on the precious metals used in the batteries, such as lithium.

A second step in the way forward is to tax every EV for road usage. Currently, road repair in the US is largely paid for with a gasoline tax. In the 1930s, the gasoline tax was introduced to pay for road usage repair. At that time, almost all vehicles had the same fuel efficiency, about 15 mpg. So, this was a very fair tax in that the more you drove, the more you used the roads, and the more tax you paid. Today, without a road usage tax on EVs, they drive on the same roads without paying their fair share of road repair. This will need to be rectified with some kind of road usage tax.

However, there is no question that electric vehicles are the way of the future. Fifty years from now, EVs will be the standard vehicle. By then, we will get most of our energy from clean wind, solar, or nuclear power. The electric grid will be a two-way grid. Homes will, in general, supply much of their own electrical needs with solar panels and the EV will be able to top off the home power on cloudy days.

Transitions are hard. This is an area where the Church can help, as the Church often has the long view in mind. After all, the Church has been around for more than 2,000 years. Perhaps the Church can bring a huge dollop of wisdom to these difficult long-range problems.

Discussion Questions

1. Transitions are hard. There are many questions, such as: Where should the public electric charge be placed? Should all churches be required to have them? Should every restaurant be required to have them? If so, how many? How should we address these questions?

2. Should the Christian Church be a strong advocate for electric vehicles or should it stay on the sidelines? Why do you think this?

3. How important is it that Christians worship together in a building? Wouldn't it be better for everyone to just stay home and save the transportation energy? Why?

Artificial Intelligence, Autonomous Vehicles, and Robots

What does the Bible say about artificial intelligence? Directly, not much. Indirectly quite a lot.

The Bible does not shy away from technology. Technology masters are first mentioned in Genesis, chapter 4.

> *20 And Adah bore Jabal. He was the father of those who dwell in tents and have livestock. 21 His brother's name was Jubal. He was the father of all those who play the harp and flute. 22 And as for Zillah, she also bore Tubal-Cain, an instructor of every craftsman in bronze and iron. (Genesis 4:20-22)*

Jabal was the master of nomadic animal husbandry. His brother, Jubal, was the master of music and musical instruments. Tubal-Cain was the master of metalwork. These three industries started thousands and thousands of years before the Roman Empire. During the Roman Empire, they used these early skills to develop oxen-driven carts and plows, horse-drawn chariots, aqueducts, water wheels, and even scaled metal armor for battle. All of these technologies were for making life safer, easier, and more productive.

Jump forward and we have made huge technological advances. We have moved from horse-drawn vehicles to internal combustion engines, to electric vehicles. In the 1970s the first artificial intelligence (AI) system was introduced into the automotive industry with the anti-lock braking system (ABS). The ABS system could automatically determine if the vehicle was spinning on a slick surface, such as ice, and automatically adjust the braking on each of the four wheels to better keep the vehicle from sliding out of control. When the ABS system kicked in, the human driver had no control over this aspect of the braking system. This is a good example of an AI system potentially saving human lives.

In the 2010s pre-autonomous vehicle systems emerged, such as the automatic emergency braking (AEB) system. This system can apply the brakes if the vehicle senses an object in its path and calculates that the human driver cannot stop in time. This could be because the human driver is not paying attention, is distracted, going too fast, or has slow reaction times. The AEB system is deemed to be superior because it is always alert, always observing, and can react more quickly. Here AI is saving human lives in a way that potentially the human, with his or her slower reaction times, cannot.

Soon, fully autonomous vehicles will be common and used because they can potentially save human lives. In the US, there are about 35,000 deaths due to automobile accidents, so these autonomous systems can potentially save many lives. An added benefit is with a fully autonomous system, the driver can do something else while commuting, such as: catching up on work, social media, or placing phone calls.

These fully autonomous vehicles make us ask a plethora of questions:

- Are they really safer?
- Will there still be accidents?
- Will they make our lives better?
- Will there be a manual override if we need to drive or take over?

The answers to these questions are all probably "yes." But they fail to ask the much deeper question; "will there be fully autonomous human robots?"

We know that we are made in God's image; "So God created man in His own image; in the image of God He created him; male and female He created them" (Genesis 1:27). We know that this goes beyond raw intelligence. It includes; passion, love, hope, and humor. Do AI machines need to have passion, love, hope, and humor?

The idea of fully autonomous human robots makes us ask another plethora of questions:

- Will they do some tasks more safely than humans?
- Will there still be accidents or costly mistakes?
- How will they make our lives better?
- Should these fully autonomous human robots have rights, like our human rights?

Perhaps the deeper question is what is the purpose, the chief end of man? The Westminster Shorter Catechism says that the chief end of man is to glorify God and enjoy Him forever.

Perhaps we should think about AI in this context. Not just, can we do it; but can it help us to glorify God and enjoy Him forever?

Discussion Questions

1. How do you think that fully autonomous vehicles or robots can make our lives better? If so, how?

2. Does the idea of fully autonomous vehicles excite you or scare you? Why?

3. Who should decide some of the ethical questions around fully autonomous vehicles or robots? How should they go about deciding these ethical questions?

4. How should the Church join in these discussions?

Artificial Intelligence and Thinking Machines

We have been using artificial intelligence as thinking machines for quite a long time. For example, search engines like Google have been around for so long that we longer search, we just "Google" the things we want to know.

Searches like "find a seafood restaurant nearby" are really quite complex. The AI system must first know where you are. Then it must define nearby. Is it less than 10 miles, or less than 30 minutes of driving? Does traffic matter? Then it must find businesses within the search radius. Then it must decide which of the businesses are seafood restaurants. For example, if there is a Chinese restaurant that specializes in seafood dishes, should this restaurant count as a seafood restaurant? Then the search engine must display the choices in some kind of order. Should they be closest to farthest, or should there be a match to your previous searches and preferences, or should the business owners have some influence in the display order? All of these decisions are defined by computer algorithms that were developed in part by human programmers.

From simple search engines, we quickly moved to recommendation engines. Companies like Amazon and Netflix specialize in these recommendation engines, as users often find that there are too many choices. When there are too many choices, some users get decision paralysis and fail to choose anything. The solution to this paralysis problem is to give fewer, but better choices. But, how do we define better choices? Machine learning algorithms are used to take a combination of what you have chosen before and what *other people like you* have chosen before. That is where it begins to get a bit scary. How does the machine decide who are *other people like me?* Is the machine using these choices to make me like other people as it attempts to make them more like me? We were taught that we were made in God's image, and not our digital neighbor's image. When do these recommendation engines go too far?

Then we moved into facial recognition. Facial recognition is used in handheld smartphones, high-end security systems, and cameras in the streets of China. China uses facial recognition cameras as a part of its social credit system that assigns scores to its citizens. These social credit scores are important in business transactions, like getting a loan or a travel visa. As with any scientific or engineering achievement, it may not be a perfect system. What happens when a facial recognition system thinks you are someone you are not? Are you again being made into the image of your digital neighbor and not your own God-given image?

Then we moved into Natural Language Processing (NLP) systems. These natural language systems attempt to understand human language, with all of its stutters and nuances, and then respond with understandable human phraseology. For example, in the early days of NLP, you could ask for the local weather. You could ask if it would be raining this afternoon. However, if you asked if you should take an umbrella, the system would fail as it had learned how to connect rainy weather with rainy clothing or accouterments.

All of these systems will improve over time and they will get better and better. Many will say that they will get to be 'more human-like.' This brings us to the big questions:

- What does it mean to be human?
- What does it mean to be made in the image of God?
- Many would say that humans were given a special helping of intelligence, passion, will to achieve, desire to create, and the ability to love, etc. Do you believe this?
- Will machines get to this same level?
- Do we want them to get to this same level?

When the machines get better will they take over some human jobs? Most certainly, as this always happens. How many buggy whip manufacturers do you know?

- A good question to ask is whether this job change is bad, good, or just a fact of technological advancement.

What does it mean that when God created us, He created us to have purposeful lives? How do we find purpose in this new technological frontier?

Discussion Questions

1. Many would say that humans were given a special helping of intelligence, passion, will to achieve, desire to create, and the ability to love, etc. What do you believe about this? How would you describe what you believe to a friend or neighbor?

2. What do you think about machines taking over some human jobs?

3. What does it mean that when God created us, He created us to have purposeful lives? How do we find purpose in this new technological frontier?

Communication and Making a Name for Ourselves

The story of the Tower Babel has several interesting lessons for us today.

> *¹ Now the whole earth had one language and one speech. ² And it came to pass, as they journeyed from the east, that they found a plain in the land of Shinar, and they dwelt there. ³ Then they said to one another, "Come, let us make bricks and bake them thoroughly." They had brick for stone, and they had asphalt for mortar. ⁴ And they said, "Come, let us build ourselves a city, and a tower whose top is in the heavens; let us make a name for ourselves, lest we be scattered abroad over the face of the whole earth."*
> *(Genesis 11:1-4)*

In this narrative, the purpose of building the tower is to "make a name for ourselves". The clear purpose is to make a tower that goes to the heavens so that we will be on top. This appears to be the same reason for social media "stars". There are people today who are famous for being famous. They have not done anything in life but be famous entertainers. They have not made any new products, not helped find a cure for cancer, nor have they helped us travel to Mars.

There is another set of people making a name for themselves, those whom we call "influencers".

Influencers have a great following on social media. Because they have a great following, they can greatly impact our way of life, our fashions, and our attitudes. Whether they recognize it or not, they are part of the great commercial marketing machine. They will only remain great influencers if they can keep up their number of followers. This puts them on a different kind of rat race, but a rat race nonetheless. They must always be looking over their shoulders at the next up-and-comer to try to stay ahead. Unfortunately, they know that they will not be influencers forever, one day, potentially very soon they will fall into obscurity.

These famous people know that their fame will die with them. As they have not really done anything, they will not leave any legacy behind. It will be as if they never existed. There is an old proverb that says; "After the game is over, the pawn and the king are put into the same box". They know that fame is very fickle and fleeting and they hate this. This knowledge unfortunately drives them to emotional and psychological depression. They often wonder why they are devoting some much effort to being famous. They also know that when their fame begins to fade many of their "friends" will desert them. They struggle to understand this as their fame makes them believe that they are really more important and better than other people.

Oddly enough God proposed a cure for this cycle of emotional and psychological depression. "Don't do it." He said:

Come, let Us go down and there confuse their language, that they may not understand one another's speech. *" So the LORD scattered them abroad from there over the face of all the earth, and they ceased building the city (Genesis 11:7-8).*

God proposed the cure using confusing language and understanding. At first blush, this seems like an odd cure to the problem of self-importance. Perhaps, the point of the story is that real, deep personal communication takes work. It takes sitting down, eye to eye, and really listening to understand the other person deeply. It cannot be done in 140 characters. In fact, for some, it takes an entire lifetime to understand the personal language of another person.

Many languages today are greatly increasing their slang words and incorporating them into their dictionaries. Ten years ago, who would have thought that LOL would stand for Laughing Out Loud instead of Lots Of Love? When used in a message of sympathy to a friend who has lost a loved one, the two meanings are quite different.

Understanding others is first and foremost not about making a name for ourselves. What do you think, are we getting better at understanding others in this day of building our own Tower of the Famous?

Discussion Questions

1. Why do you think that the people in Babel built the tower? Why was it so important to build a tower that went up to the heavens?

2. Do you think we are still doing this kind of thing today? If so, give an example or two.

3. Understanding others is first and foremost not about making a name for ourselves. What do you think, are we getting better at understanding others in this day of building our own Tower of the Famous? How could we get better at it?

4. Do you think language is getting more complex, and difficult to understand? Why or why not?

The Flow of Information

The Tower of Babel narrative has another great lesson about the power of communication.

⁵ But the LORD came down to see the city and the tower which the sons of men had built. ⁶ And the LORD said, "Indeed the people are one and they all have one language, and this is what they begin to do; now nothing that they propose to do will be withheld from them. ⁷ Come, let Us go down and there confuse their language, that they may not understand one another's speech." ⁸ So the LORD scattered them abroad from there over the face of all the earth, and they ceased building the city. ⁹ Therefore its name is called Babel, because there the LORD confused the language of all the earth; and from there the LORD scattered them abroad over the face of all the earth. (Genesis 11:5-9)

The people of the earth were trying to build a tall tower so that it would reach heaven itself. Perhaps they would be able to dethrone God Himself, for nothing they proposed would be withheld from them. Was God worried that He might be dethroned? Probably not. Was He worried for us, probably so. With our technology, we can do wonderful things, as well as horribly evil things.

A very interesting example of this is the Gutenberg printing press. Johannes Gutenberg invented the movable-type printing press around 1440. The Gutenberg printing press changed society forever. With this press, for the first time, the world stepped into the era of mass communication. Before the moveable-type press, only the elite had books and could read. Before the moveable-type printing press, each page had to be etched by hand, which was very time-consuming. The moveable-type printing press allowed the emerging middle class to not only read but to print up their own information.

The scientific world was generally excited about this invention. The press allowed them to share their ideas and theories much more widely. It allowed them to print textbooks to begin to teach others about their scientific theories. They saw the spread of knowledge as a good thing. They were not worried, initially, about poor scientific works being printed, because who would do that?

However, the Roman Catholic Church did not see the printing press as a good thing. Before the printing press, only priests had Bibles. They were the only ones who could read so they were the only ones who could interpret the Bible for everyday life. In the early 1500s, Martin Luther saw the wonderful value of the printing press. He first translated the New Testament into German and then, using the printing press, made the Bible available for the people of the Church in their language and not just the priests. His translation of the New Testament sold over 5,000 copies in just two weeks. By around 1525, Luther's writing accounted for almost a third of all of the books sold in Germany.

The printing press was of course just a forerunner to the world-wide-web or the Internet as we know it today. By using the Internet, almost anyone can publish an article for everyone to read. The Internet can even translate an article from one language to another for us. The Internet has forced us to think more deeply about communications and information, but these questions are the same ones that were being asked in the era of the printing press.

The printing press raised very important questions about communication and information.

1. Should anyone be allowed to publish information to others around the world?
2. Should the elite monitor the flow of information to guard against the spread of misinformation?
3. How is misinformation defined?
4. What should be the speed and spread of new information?
5. Can information spread too quickly?
6. Is speed more important than accuracy?

It has been over five hundred years since the use of the printing press and we still struggle with these questions above. Are we any closer to answers to these questions?

Discussion Questions

1. Should anyone be allowed to publish information to others around the world? Why or why not?

2. Should the elite monitor the flow of information to guard against the spread of misinformation? Why or why not?

3. How should misinformation be defined?

4. What should be the speed and spread of new information? How should it be monitored?

Should it be slowed down?

5. Can information spread too quickly? Why or why not?

6. Is speed more important than accuracy? How do we deal with the validity and importance of information?

How to Best Store Information

For those who study information storage, this has always been an important question; *How to best store information*? They are not asking about storing information for a few years, for a few decades, but for hundreds of years.

In today's digital age, we think that storing information digitally is the best way to store information. It is convenient, easy to compress, and easy to retrieve – at least for a while. However, perhaps a short history of information storage would be helpful.

In the 1950s magnetic tapes were introduced. They were thin strips of plastic coated with magnetic material. They could store a few megabytes of data. They needed reels for the tape and special tape-reading machines.

In the 1970s floppy disk drives were invented. They brought easy and convenient storage to the masses. The floppy drive was small enough to fit into your shirt pocket and it could store a whopping 1.44 MB. A big improvement.

In the 1980s solid-state drives were first introduced. They became popular with the advent of the USB thumb drive. The Universal Serial Bus (USB) was envisioned to be a standard that would last for many years. The USB drive has gone through several major iterations, but it can still be used on most computers.

In the 2000s Cloud storage was introduced. It was argued that it is too inefficient for everyone to store their own information. It should all be stored together in massive Cloud storage systems.

In this short 50 years of history, what lessons can be learned?

- Even if magnetic tapes or floppy disk drivers were still around, no one would be able to read them. This is an important lesson, storage and reading of information must go hand in hand. Data that cannot be read is not useful data. Think of all of that data on floppy disks that will never be read.
- Digital storage does not last forever. Even solid-state drives have a finite number of read and write cycles before they begin to deteriorate. They can also be damaged by electronic interference or even gamma-ray radiation from the sun.
- Cloud storage is wonderful in that the average person does not have to worry about it, until... What happens if the Cloud storage system fails? What happens if it is hacked or erased? What happens if my personal data is not kept secure but is cross-referenced for purposes outside of my purview?
- How will any of these storage devices be read a hundred years from now?

Oddly enough, the only storage devices that have lasted hundreds of years or even a few thousand years are:

- Impressions placed in clay
- Writings on paper or parchment (animal skin)

The clear advantage of this type of storage is that it has been shown to last a long time. The clear disadvantage of this type of storage is that it can only save small bits of information.

It is interesting to note that when God gave Moses the written commandments, He wrote the commandments with His finger on the stone.

Then the LORD delivered to me two tablets of stone written with the finger of God, and on them were all the words which the LORD had spoken to you on the mountain from the midst of the fire in the day of the assembly. (Deuteronomy 9:10)

While these specific tablets seem to be lost in the passage of time if they were found today, they could still be read.

In 1977 the Voyager satellite was launched into the deep reaches of outer space with a message about the life and culture of Earth. In this case, it was a gold-plated copper disk with an inscribed message. The message contained words, images, and analog sounds. The disk should last a long time. The question is, will anyone ever read it?

Therefore, the tradeoff seems to be saving a lot (terabytes) of data for tens of years and then moving it to another storage system, ad infinite, or saving small bits of data with very "primitive" systems. What do you think will win out in the end?

Discussion Questions

1. Why do you think that long-term storage of information is important? What of your personal information should be stored for a thousand years?

2. Do you think that we will come up with a better digital system that will last for hundreds of years? Why or why not?

3. If you were in charge of the Voyager satellite system, what message would you have encoded on the disk?

4. How do we ensure that people are reading the Bible a thousand years from now?

Concluding Thoughts

We know that we are wonderfully created with intelligence, wills, and passions. We know that the world is also wonderfully made, as we see this in sunsets, starry nights, and roaring oceans. While science seems to be all about the latest recent discovery, there is much that can be learned from studying the Ancients.

For example, we know that we are all still learning and that no one can know everything. We also know that much of life is based on faith. For example, when we are facing a difficult problem, we often rely on Occam's Razor "The simplest explanation is often the best." We all take this as a good way to live, perhaps even as a scientific truth, even though it has never been proven, nor can it be. We take it on reasonable faith. We should not be afraid to live our lives based on reasonable or verifiable faith.

Much of real, everyday life is difficult to live without some understanding of God. He brings a foundation of right and wrong, morality, ways to live a good life, and a purpose for life. These foundations are difficult to hold on to if we believe that we came from the primordial goop and we are no different from the amoeba. Perhaps we should bring a God-centered view into more of our life and science discussions.

Today we live in a technology-driven world. However, it is important to sometimes take a step back from our technology and think about what really matters in life.

Hopefully, you can continue to use some of these Reflections and questions to help you ponder the deepest questions of life.

TS Taylor

Prayer to Accept Jesus

If you found this reflections book helpful and you felt God tugging at your heart, you can respond to the Holy Spirit right now.

If you have never accepted Jesus as your own personal Lord and Savior, you can do that with a simple prayer.

You can pray something like this:

"Thank you, God, for loving me and sending your Son to die for my sins. I sincerely repent of my sins, and receive Christ as my personal savior. Now, as your child, I turn my entire life over to you. Amen."

If you have any questions, you can reach out to me at:

tstaylor.devotionals@gmail.com

May God bless you on your own spiritual journey.

Other Books by TS Taylor

Life-Changing Devotionals

The Love and Mercy of God as Seen in Jonah, Job, and Joseph

Flight to Freedom, Laws to Live By, How to Worship

Exodus Devotionals

High and Lifted Up – Is God Still Engaged in His World?

Isaiah Devotionals

Walk with Jesus and His Followers

Matthew Devotional

Life Applications from Romans

Romans Devotional

Other Books by TS Taylor

Scientific Faith

How to Bridge the Gap Between Faith and Science – Small Group Study Book

Acknowledgments

I wish to thank my class at the Church of the Apostles in Atlanta, Georgia. They worked through much of this material, as we learned from the Scriptures together.

Soli Deo Gloria

Made in the USA
Columbia, SC
25 September 2023